T0063174

Other books by author
*The Laughing Christ*
*El's Rae: A Memoir*
*Homeward Bound: Meditations for Your Journey*
*Be Still and Know*
*The Peaceful Silence*
*Concordance of The Aquarian Gospel of Jesus the Christ*
*Home to the Light*
*The Beckoning Light*
*Divination Through the Ages*

Teachings of Archangel Gabriel and Jesus the Christ printed with permission

Section One: *AV/KJV*
Section Two: *The Good News Bible*

# THE
# HIGH ROAD HOME

Rev. Ellen Wallace Douglas

Order this book online at www.trafford.com
or email orders@trafford.com

Most Trafford titles are also available at major online book retailers.

KJV
Scripture quotations marked KJV are from the Holy Bible, King James Version
(Authorized Version). First published in 1611. Quoted from the KJV Classic
Reference Bible, Copyright © 1983 by The Zondervan Corporation.

Printed in the United States of America.

ISBN: 978-1-4907-4198-7 (sc)
ISBN: 978-1-4907-4197-0 (e)

*Trafford rev. 07/15/2014*

 www.trafford.com
North America & international
toll-free: 1 888 232 4444 (USA & Canada)
fax: 812 355 4082

To all humankind, Homeward bound

*Call to me, and I will answer you; I will tell you wonderful and marvelous things that you know nothing about.* Jer. 33:3

# CONTENTS

# PREFACE

In October of 1987 a spirit entity came to bring wisdom to the church congregation at Trinity Temple of the Holy Spirit, in Albany, NY. When asked his name he said we should call him Lucas. Four years later he said he was Archangel Gabriel. He used 'Lucas' for a time because Reverend Penny A. Donovan (founding Pastor of Trinity Temple) could not accept the idea that she was worthy to channel an archangel, although she was a natural medium and channeled spirit often in her Psychic Development classes.

In the ensuing years, Gabriel visited our group of spiritual seekers, at various local venues in the Capital District. The seminars were advertised. Everyone was welcome. He said he would come twelve years, and he did; from 1987-1999. His visitations (all-day seminars) took place bi-monthly. Jesus the Christ also came - from 1995-1999 - through Rev. Penny, this devout and gifted channel, prepared by spirit to do so.

After hearing all this wisdom of the ages, I was inspired to become a writer and pass on his lessons to all spiritual seekers. My previous books include references to Gabriel and his teachings. Finally, it was made clear to me that I should also pass on Gabriel's interpretation of various passages in Scripture. That is the focus and content of this book. I searched all my handwritten notes from the seminars I attended for Bible quotations noted by Gabriel. I never missed an all-day seminar locally, but Gabriel did present at other locations, including Las Vegas and Lilly Dale, NY.

Chapters One through Ten give Gabriel's interpretation of various parts of the New Testament. The last four chapters contain Gabriel's interpretation of *The Revelation of John,* which has been a conundrum to humanity - clergy and lay people alike - since written. How blessed I was to hear it; how blessed I am to pass it on; how blessed are you to continue spreading this wondrous truth. Gabriel instructed Rev. Penny to have someone read *Revelation* from the *Good News Bible,* and he would give the interpretation paragraph by paragraph. Rev. Penny asked me to read. I was ecstatic!

It is certain that Archangel's teachings will be distributed throughout the world in the coming centuries. As a matter of fact, Gabriel told us that eleven Master Teachers came to various places on Earth the same years that he came, to bring to all humanity the same message; the truth of our being - that we are *all* children of God and must wake up to our innate divinity, and live from the Lord God of our Being.

The chapters are presented in chronological order of the seminars, because any other method seemed unnecessary, and would be a complex and challenging endeavor.

Gabriel and Jesus *always* answered questions of the audience. Only occasionally are Question and Answer sessions referred to, and then because the content is deemed highly significant and cogent to the topic. Gabriel mentions some words more than once. Only the first time used is the word defined.

Regarding chapters 11-14, the interpretation of *Revelation,* Gabriel said, "It is the holiness of the story of humankind's journey back unto the Father." All of the words in these four chapters are direct quotations of Gabriel. Paraphrasing is not used, for it would be blasphemous to do so, with such sacred and enlightening wisdom given us by an archangel. However, quotation marks are not used for the following reasons:

Gabriel sometimes digresses from the topic.

Ellipses would permeate the text.

Many quotation marks hinder the flow of content.

Because Archangel Gabriel presented the interpretation of *Revelation* in in two full days, the original typed transcript totals 180 pages. Chapters 11-14 of this volume have been reduced to only about 35 pages. All symbolism is given, but much detail has been omitted, as well as nearly all the question and answer sessions. Also, the passages of the

Bible read by Rev. Ellen are not included. It is recommended that the reader familiarize himself with the *Good News Bible* before reading, or read the Bible alongside this book. It is suggested the reader know about numerology and the chakras, since Gabriel refers to them frequently in the last four chapters. He also mentions the kundalini.

All Bible quotations are italicized, in respect for the Good Book and its sacred contents. It is not known why Gabriel referred to the King James translation in all his previous lessons, and then referred to the *Good News Bible* when interpreting *Revelation*.

All italics and punctuation marks are author's, as deemed appropriate.

Refer to the Appendix for list of seminars presented in the text.

Regarding the title *The High Road Home*, the word 'high' is intended to mean 'above all else' such as is the spirit world. 'Road' as a well-defined path to travel and 'Home' is Heaven. It is our true Home, for Gabriel told us that "Heaven is our natural habitat".

With deep and abiding gratitude, I hereby acknowledge the editorial input of Marylou Krywe and Grace Abbott.

# INTRODUCTION

Throughout his lessons, Archangel Gabriel quoted the Bible, but never gave the chapter and verse. Sometimes the Bible quotation did not seem to 'fit' the seminar's title. This was due in part to Gabriel's habit of digressing briefly from the topic. As for the Bible as a whole, he said,

"*The Old Testament* is the unenlightened history; without knowledge.

"*The New Testament* (if understood properly) is Jesus' teachings. [It is] the story of the soul of mankind.

"*A Course in Miracles* is the same as the New Testament, but with current wording."

In other seminars Gabriel noted, regarding the Bible, that all references to reincarnation were purged from the original writing of the Bible. Also all references to the many women who followed Jesus were deleted. It is written in the male gender because men wrote the Bible, and it was then a male-dominated society.

The two comments about scripture Gabriel made which shocked me the most:

1. 'Jesus Christ, only son of God' originally was written 'Jesus Christ, son of the only God'.
2. Jesus did not suffer on the cross, because he held his consciousness within his Spirit Self, which he reached in Gethsemane when he said,

"Father, my Father! All things are possible for you. Take this cup of suffering away from me. Yet not what I want, but what you want." Mark 14:36

At different times, Gabriel supplied us with two revised versions of the 23rd Psalm. One is the female version, which can be found in *Sitting at*

*Gabriel's Feet,* by the author, in the chapter "All My Mothers". This is the other:

The Lord is my shepherd, I have no desire beyond this.
He maketh me to lie down in green pastures of abundance;
He leads me beside still waters of His peace.
He cleanses my soul of all error.
He leads me in paths of righteousness by Divine Will
For the purpose of At-One-Ment.
Yea, though I walk through the valley of perception
I will fear no error
For Thou art with me. Thy Love and Thy Truth,
They comfort me.
Thou preparest a table of beauty and joy before me.
Thou anointest my head with understanding;
My cup runneth over.
Surely goodness and mercy shall follow me
All the days of my life,
And I will dwell in the Consciousness of God forever.
© Penny Donovan 2000

# CHRONOLOGIC
# SEMINARS

# 1988

September 1988, untitled
*Bible*
*And then shall appear the sign of the Son of man in heaven: and then shall all the tribes of the earth mourn, and they shall see the Son of man coming in the clouds of heaven with power and great glory.* Matt. 24:30

*Archangel Gabriel*
The New Age is upon you. The clouds are [your] error thoughts.

---------------------------------------------------------------------

*Bible*
*And be not conformed to this world: but be ye transformed by the renewing f your mind, that ye may prove what is that good, and acceptable, and perfect, will of God.*
Rom. 12:2

*Archangel Gabriel*
New energy (with the New Age) and what grows with it is transformed; what grows not with it is destroyed, by earthquakes etc.

---------------------------------------------------------------------

*Bible*
*Then shall two be in the field; the one shall be taken, and the other left.*
Matt.24:40

*Archangel Gabriel*
The taken one has old awareness; unwilling to accept new energy. The other is with Christ; out of old awareness and in the change with new energy.

------------------------------------------------------------------

*Bible*
*And as he sat upon the mount of Olives, the disciples came unto him privately, saying, Tell us, when shall these things be? And what shall be the sign of thy coming, and of the end of the world?* Matt. 24:3

*Archangel Gabriel*
You are *in Revelation.*

*author*
This first day-long seminar Gabriel stunned us with the fact we are now living in the time predicted by the *Revelation to John.* See chapters 11-14.

------------------------------------------------------------------

*Bible*
*And I saw a new heaven and a new earth: for the first heaven and the first earth were passes away; and there was no more sea.* Rev. 21:1

*Archangel Gabriel*
This is the awareness of the livingness of the Lord God of your Being.

------------------------------------------------------------------

*Bible*
*Heaven and earth shall pass away, but my words shall not pass away.* Matt. 24:35; Mark 13:31

*Archangel Gabriel*
The earth, as you know it, will disappear.

------------------------------------------------------------------

*Bible*
*And he answered and said unto them, I tell you that, if these should hold their peace, the stones would immediately cry out.* Matt.19:40

*Archangel Gabriel*
Jesus took his body with him because he learned how at other planets.
The rocks knew the Christ.

------------------------------------------------------------

*Bible*
*And God said, Let us make man in our image, after our likeness; and let*
*them have dominion over the fish of the sea, and over the fowl of the air,*
*and over the cattle, and over all the earth, and over every creeping thing that*
*creepeth upon the earth.* Gen. 1:26

*Archangel Gabriel*
'Dominion' does not mean to rule over. It means to be in harmony with.
Lift up your consciousness to all kingdoms of life. Speak to a piece of
fruit. If you do not mean what you say, plants know; animals know.
Speak from your heart, not your mouth. In this New Age the Christ
consciousness is coming again to teach you through the twelve of us.

*Author*
Gabriel told us that besides himself, eleven Master Teachers also came
simultaneously to various places on earth to teach all humankind one
lesson: Wake up to the fact you are all Sons of God; divine by nature; and
live from the Lord God of your being.

------------------------------------------------------------

*Bible*
*Having eyes, see ye not? And having ears hear ye not? and do ye not remember?*

*Archangel Gabriel*
If you have the eyes to see and the heart to know, you would never hurt a
livingness… Carnivorous animals need not be carnivorous.
Human error thoughts created them.

*Author*
A football was in the room (at another seminar) and Gabriel asked what
it was. When told it was the skin of a pig, he said, 'Was the animal asked

for its hide?' We laughed; Gabriel did not. Then we realized the truth of Gabriel's words - all life is sacred.

-------------------------------------------------------------------------------

*Bible*
*But wilt thou know, O vain man, that faith without works is dead?*
James 2:20

*Archangel Gabriel*
Live your faith… You have a wonderful knowingness within you waiting to be set free. I live my prayers, my meditations and my God.
This is the meaning of The Lord's Prayer:

*Our Father* - Shows the oneness of all life.

*Who art in heaven* - unspeakable joy; the perfect state of one who dwells within.

*Holy be thy name.* - We are all holy. All creatures are holy.

*Thy kingdom come* - The livingness within to come forth.

*Thy will be done on earth* - Holiness within you willing your highest good. Come to earth: be manifest in form.

*As it is in heaven* - Joy and Light on earth.

*Give us daily bread* - Not just food. Let us always be aware of Thy truth. Feed our consciousness and lift us up.

*Forgive our debts* - Release us from the karma that we create.

*As we forgive* - the capacity to forgive self; to accept forgiveness. No one can do to you what is worthy of lasting forever.

*Lead us not into temptation* - God will not lead us into temptation. He said, 'Lead us in the paths of light and understanding.'

*Deliver us from evil* - Evil is your own error thoughts that lead you astray.

*Thine is the kingdom* - We all are part of it. When you are lifted up in consciousness forever and ever and ever.

This is prayer. Meditation is acceptance of; knowingness of, oneness with God. Contemplate yourself; not a candle. This is the greatest contemplation… contemplate the wonderment of you - not your body; the inner you that only you know. Know the unspeakable beauty of you, for you are wondrously made by God. If you could see your own beauty, you would be amazed. You are a truth set free - limitless; boundless. You are love, for you are of God and He loves you… Praise God by living all you are; being all you are; loving all you are.

---

*Bible*
*Believeth thou not that I am in the Father, and the Father in me? The words that I speak unto you I speak not of myself: but the Father that dwelleth in me, he doeth the works.* John 14:10

*Archangel Gabriel*
You must let our Father doeth the works in you. First thing in the morning say, 'I call you forth in the utmost of love, that I might go forth among my fellow beings and radiate that which I am. I am the God of me.'

Don't let your radiance be brought down by others - some will love you; some will not. You are limited only by your own ability to think you are limited.

---

*Bible*
*But seek ye first the kingdom of God, and his righteousness; and all these things shall be added unto you.* Matt. 6:33

*Archangel Gabriel*

When you first love God for the sake of love, all things are added unto you. An inner knowing is required, then all objects you desire will be yours. Why love the smell of the smoke instead of the warmth of the fire? Why taste the crumbs on the floor when the banquet awaits you?

*Author*

Gabriel told us that 'want' and 'need' both imply lack. When we 'desire' something, it comes from (de) the Father (sire).

---

*Bible*

*I and my Father are one.* John 10:30

*Archangel Gabriel*

When you see me, you see the Father. [It is] meant to bring you together; not fearful and separate, as old priests taught - to control you.

# CHAPTER TWO

# 1989

1/15/89 Female Energy
(author note: this was a two-day seminar, but Gabriel quoted scripture only in the second day, part two)

*Bible*
*Blessed are the poor in spirit: for theirs is the kingdom of heaven.*
*Blessed are they that mourn: for they shall be comforted.* Matt. 5:3-4

*Archangel Gabriel*
Blessed are the poor in spirit because they are *unaware* of their blessedness.
Blessed are mourners because they are *unaware* of the Comforter.

*Author*
How could we be unaware of our blessedness? Some blessings come suddenly and openly. We recognize and acknowledge them immediately. Others are unrecognized for years, and in retrospect we identify the blessings. The job interviews that were unsuccessful and we thought God was not listening; then the perfect job was ours. It reminds me of the lesson Gabriel gave us about our angels and how they work to bring about our requests/prayers. The job we finally got was simply not available before it became ours. Picture, if you will, your angels – and we each have 144,000 of them, according to Gabriel - asking to be shown all such jobs, in a specified area, and the likelihood of one of them being available in the near future. Can we begin to imagine such a man-made computer? This explains the time factor and exemplifies how our angels work for us. It also confirms the biblical phrase 'Ask and ye shall receive.'

When I was shopping for a new car during the twelve years in which Gabriel visited, he told me that three times my angels found the vehicle I sought, but three times my thinking the deal would fail made it fail!

Besides the lesson in angelic workings, here was a lesson in how powerful our thoughts are.

Turning again to scripture we find: And all things, whatsoever ye shall ask in prayer, believing, ye shall receive. Matt. 21:22 we must not beg God for our desires. He knows them all. As His beloved children He will answer all prayers. The time in which He grants them may not be according to our timetable, but He will answer. Do you honestly believe that God would give you anything but a blessing? Have you not seen, or experienced, a seeming tragedy turn into a blessing? The beloved archangel told us that huge forest fires bring forth new vegetation and new soil. Tsunamis and floods teach us a lesson in brotherhood as we pull together in recovery efforts. As mourners we are blessed by the Comforter, whether we are aware of Him or not.

-------------------------------------------------------------------

6/24/89 Multi-dimensions of Consciousness
*Bible*
*Consider the lilies of the field, how they grow; they toil not, neither do they spin.* Matt. 6:28

*Archangel Gabriel*
All life is inter-connected unto a state of consciousness. Each level of life is ruled by a higher level, up to the Father.

*Author*
This is exemplified by our ability to have inter-species communication. Communication with the plant kingdom was demonstrated by the gardeners at Findhorn, in Scotland. Many individuals talk to their canine and feline pets; some talk to their flowers and plants. Life in any form is able to communicate with other life forms. When we study whale's sounds we will know what they are saying to us. When we learn how to communicate with all terrestrial species, we will know that then we can communicate with beings in space - extraterrestrials. It is unfortunate that when humans think of life on other planets, and the possibility of the residents visiting us, we assume they want to destroy us. How long will it take for us to accept the idea that they are more advanced and

might want to teach us what they know? Those from other planets have much to teach us, for Earth is the only planet where disease and death are still practiced. Gabriel told us this.

---

*Bible*
*For if ye love them which love you, what reward have ye? Matt. 5:46*

*Archangel Gabriel*
Remember, you were once where they [those you judge] are. It is the ego which says 'an eye for an eye'. Once an individual wants to be free, legions of angels will help to free him.

*Author*
What strikes me about Matthew's question is that it implies we *ought* to have rewards. Love is its own reward, but we deny ourselves that love, that reward, when we judge others, and continue into resentments. To resent is to re-feel and in our unwillingness to forgive, we deny ourselves the reward of love. The freedom that forgiveness offers is a freedom that we already have but lack awareness of, when we judge.

---

*Bible*
*For where two or three are gathered together in my name, there am I in the midst of them (Matt. 18:20)*

*Archangel Gabriel*
When Jesus said this, he meant where two or more *agree,* the power is there; the power of the Holy Spirit. Energy is like jello; it forms what your divine will seeks. Withdraw from what you do not want; give energy to what you do want. Your thinking is making your world and you can change your world anytime. The spoken word is very powerful - for it is the expression of your thoughts, it is a commitment of our energy; it is a declaration of your will.

*Author*
We have the capacity to change our world if we choose, and we choose when we pray *Thy Kingdom come. Thy will be done in earth, as it is in Heaven.* Matt. 6:10

---

*Bible*
*And he commanded the multitude to sit down on the grass, and took the five loaves, and the two fishes, and looking up to heaven, he blessed, and brake, and gave the loaves to the disciples, and the disciples to the multitude. And they did all eat, and were filled: and they took up of the fragments that remained twelve baskets full. Matt. 14:19-20*

*Archangel Gabriel*
You ought to say, 'Thank you Father for that which we have', not 'please can we have'. Also, everyone there had some bread stashed for the trip. No one traveled then without necessary provisions.

---

8/1/89 Karma and Grace
*Bible*
*Whatsoever you have done unto the least of these, you have done it unto me.* Matt. 25:40

*Archangel Gabriel*
When you tear apart a flower, you tear apart the beingness of life. Life is precious everywhere. It is an integral part of you. You do not revere that which you have.

---

*Bible*
*Judge not, that ye be not judged.* Matt. 7:1
*Ye shall know the truth and the truth shall make you free.* (8:32)

*Archangel Gabriel*
Ask yourself, 'What shall my day be?' Listen to your inner self. Release one person, in love; cherish him as he is.

-----------------------------------------------------------------------

10/28/89 How to Live in the Days to Come
*Bible*
*Only with thine eyes shalt thou behold and see the reward of the wicked.* Psalm 91:8

*Archangel Gabriel*
All your needs will be supplied, if you work for it, using what is given you - knowledge, supplies. No matter what condition your world is in, you are in the valley of peace. All things begin with thought. Light is vibration of thought, only slower. Thought, to light, to movement. The sun is pure light; pure energy, esoteric ness. The sun gave birth to all the planets.

*Author*
Our mortal eyes see what we choose to see. From our Higher Self we envision only good; only positive.

-----------------------------------------------------------------------

*Bible*
*I am the vine, ye are the branches.* John 15:5

*Archangel Gabriel*
This is the love aspect. We [angels] know everyone as part of love. The vine is mass consciousness. The further from the vine, the more individual you become. You all have yucky days because you have tapped into a negative idea: sickness, poverty, etc. To be loving you represent all love. Love is the desire to give, nurture, please, sacrifice.

If God loves you He desires to give you abundance. *Fear not, little flock; for it is your Father's good pleasure to give you the kingdom.* (12:32) True wealth is health, family, friends. Gold is the only metal that can hold emotion (love) forever. It is the universal symbol of wealth. It is one of the purest physical manifestations of the Father. There is poverty on Earth because gold doesn't flow. It is hoarded by dictators. Those who control gold control love. You think you are free. You have given your power away; money runs you. Love is the essence of your being; love has to be expressed. Poverty is not equal to godliness. Who owns your home? Your car? Your food? You are all slaves. Wake up! See your freedom as an illusion. Democracy is an illusion. You need not fear Russia; weapons.

-----------------------------------------------------------------------

*Bible*
*It is more blessed to give than receive* (Acts 20:35)

*Archangel Gabriel*
It is *as* blessed to give as to receive.

-----------------------------------------------------------------------

*Bible*
*And be not conformed to this world: but be ye transformed by the renewing of your mind, that ye may prove what is that good, and acceptable, and perfect, will of God.* Romans 12:2

*Archangel Gabriel*
Do not fear rejection of another and you will not fear yourself. You become new from the renewing of your mind. It is from the new Heaven of *you* that your new world will come.

*Author*
There must be a renewing of our minds before we can prove, and become the Will of God. We never have to prove we are worthy of love. We never have to prove what we are. We don't need guilt or remorse – and without them all fears will disappear. From this new Heaven of us a new world will come. It will come as the result of this renewing of our mind; that we may prove that good, acceptable and perfect Will of God.

-----------------------------------------------------------------------

11/9/89 What the Will Power is
*Bible*
*Unto the woman he said, I will greatly multiply thy sorrow and thy conception; in sorrow thou shalt bring forth children.* Gen. 3:16

*Archangel Gabriel*
In the scriptures an allegory is told of God pronouncing a curse upon Adam and Eve. For Eve (the feminine - subconscious) He said she would birth in great pain. This is symbolic of the truth that when the God within is denied, all bringing forth will be through the pain of trial and error. No longer can you perceive yourselves as the gods that you are and therefore the will of you has fallen under the dominance of the ego, who is in error.

-----------------------------------------------------------------------

*Bible*
*In the sweat of thy face shalt thou eat bread, till thou return unto the ground.* Gen. 3:19

*Archangel Gabriel*
For Adam (the male - conscious mind; action) He [God] proclaimed him to work; by the sweat of his brow would he bring forth his food and shelter. No longer able to be guided directly by the Lord God of his being, he, through his ego, perceived his world to be one of struggle and labor. In truth, the Father never cursed anyone. It was the ego, with its limited perception, that did the deed. The power of your will is your creative ability, and when you cleanse your subconscious mind, and align your will with the Father by knowing His will for you is ever, ever, for good - and that you have the ability to call forth that good at any time - then you will find yourself receiving the good that is ever waiting your bidding. Beloved of God, be at peace. You are loved grandly.

# CHAPTER THREE

# 1991

2/16/91 Ascension and transcendence.

*Archangel Gabriel*
The *Old Testament* is the unenlightened history; without knowledge.

The *New Testament* (if understood properly) is Jesus' teachings; [it is] the story of the soul of mankind.

*A Course in Miracles* is the same as the New Testament, but with current wording.

- - - - - - - - - - - - - - - - - - - - - - - - - - - - - - - - - - - - - - - - - - - - - -

3/23/91 Decisions: What are They Really?
*Bible*
*Thou shalt have no other gods before me... Thou shalt not make unto thee any graven image... Thou shalt not bow down thyself to them... Thou shalt not take the name of the Lord thy God in vain... Honour thy father and thy mother... Thou shalt not kill... Thou shalt not commit adultery... Thou shalt not steal... Thou shalt not bear false witness... Thou shalt not covet...* Ex. 20:3-17

*Archangel Gabriel*
Men went to a mountain and meditated and chanted. They were visited by space beings (who they thought to be gods), who put into their consciousness a higher way of life. The barbaric way of living needed laws to teach that everything is by natural law.

- - - - - - - - - - - - - - - - - - - - - - - - - - - - - - - - - - - - - - - - - - - - - -

5/25/91 Vibrations
Those who read/hear the lessons from Archangel Gabriel may assume that those twelve years sitting at his feet were somber. Not so. There were many moments of joy and laughter in his presence. In this seminar he mentioned the fall of man – the Garden of Eden – "Was not due to the apple, but the pear (pair) on the ground. You thought you could separate from God, and you invented guilt, pain, and death".

*Bible*
*When the unclean spirit is gone out of a man, he walketh through dry places, seeking rest, and findeth none.*

*Then he saith, I will return unto my house from whence I came out; and when he is come, he findeth it empty, swept, and garnished.*

*Then goeth he, and taketh with himself seven other spirits more wicked than himself, and they enter in ad dwell there; and the last state of that man is worse than the first.* Matt. 12: 43-45

*Archangel Gabriel*
If [when] you cast out negativity, you *must* replace it with positive, or the negative will return many fold.

-------------------------------------------------------------------------

8/10/91 Earth Changes; Cleansing and Healing
*Bible*
*But I say unto you, Love your enemies, bless them that curse you, do good to them that hate you, and pray for them which despitefully use you, and persecute you;* Matt. 5:44; Luke 6:27

*Archangel Gabriel*
One of the challenges you will be meeting - in the days to come - is to love past appearances. You don't have to love what a person does, or what they say, or what they represent. You can dislike or even hate what another does, but it is very important for your soul to love the person and not the deed, or the words, or their affiliation.

*Author*
When we recognize the lesson presented to us by our seeming enemy, we learn and appreciate the blessing therein.

-------------------------------------------------------------------

*Bible*
*Therefore the Lord God sent him forth from the Garden of Eden, to till the ground from whence he was taken.* Gen 3:23

*Archangel Gabriel*
And so [in] the soul of you is the memory of your idea of separating yourself from God.... which is depicted in the allegory of the Garden of Eden. That part of you which is made in the image and likeness of God has never separated itself from the Source. Only in your perception have you drawn away from that which is you and that which is God intertwined.

-------------------------------------------------------------------

*Bible*
*Go to the ant, thou sluggard; consider her ways, and be wise.* Prov. 6:6

*Archangel Gabriel*
One of the great teachers on earth is the ant —that humble little insect which invades your homes and gets into your cookie jars. Its lesson is how to live in a community. They work cooperatively for their survival. No ant goes off to live by itself - even if it doesn't get along with its parents!

-------------------------------------------------------------------

Archangel Gabriel took questions at every seminar. At this seminar, a question was asked which strikes at the heart of Christianity:

Q. Is the Second Coming of Christ near?
A. It tis. But it is not in the form of a single individual. It is the Christ awareness of everyone upon the Earth. The Christ awareness has been delegated to the Christian faith and it appears to be unto that only. Well,

it isn't! The Christ awareness is non-denominational. You don't have to be a professed Christian to have the Christ awareness. It is simply that aspect of you which knows its connection with God, and lives it.

And it doesn't matter whether you are Christian or Jew or Islamic, or what you are. Everyone has that Christ awareness. You can call it something else if you want to. Connecting with Divine Mind… being made one with all life. You can name it anything you want to, but the bottom line of it is that it is the love of God made manifest in man. And that is what it is. And that is what is coming. That is what has already begun to come. And that is The Second Coming.

------------------------------------------------------------------------

## 9/28/91 The Fatherhood of God; the Brotherhood of Man
*Bible*
*He that believeth on me, the works that I do shall he do also; and greater works than these shall he do; because I go unto my Father.* John 14:12

*Archangel Gabriel*
Jesus came to teach you about your Godness. He came to show you how it is done. He did not come to start a new religion. Remove your other gods:
ego (on a daily altar of fear)
doubt
self-deception
denial (lack)

------------------------------------------------------------------------

*Bible*
*Neither shall they say, Lo, here! or, lo, there! for, behold, the kingdom of God is within you.* Luke 17:21

*Archangel Gabriel*
You are the out-picturing of your attitude toward God and your function. (your ego says you should suffer). The action of God - the idea for desire. The repose of God - allow the stillness to build desire, then

take the next action (idea). During the repose stage, have no negative thoughts. Meditate: 'My desires are out-picturing. I know my good is here.'... all material possessions are nothing without spirit abundance of consciousness that supplies your every need - physical, mental, spiritual.

------------------------------------------------------------

### Bible
*Therefore judge nothing before the time, until the Lord come, who both will bring to light the hidden things of darkness, and will make manifest the counsels of the hearts: and then shall every man have praise of God. I Cor. 4: 5*

### Archangel Gabriel
You should be fearless. Know that nothing can harm you, physical or emotional. Familiarity forms a bond. You make the same mistakes over and over. You love it to repitition. All of your fear is fear of the unknown, and you stay with the pain. Recognize that you created it, therefore you can uncreate it. Choose the way of the Christ. Jesus could raise his awareness to a stillness in body and mind.

Meditate - go past thought, observing a pulsation of life which is *you*.

### Author
Gabriel differentiated between being fearless and saying 'I am not afraid of anything'. In that statement we imply that there are things to fear. We need to remember that nothing can harm us. We need to choose the way of Christ

------------------------------------------------------------

### Bible
*The light of the body is the eye: if therefore thine eye be single, thy whole body shall be full of light. Matt. 6:22; Luke 11:34*

### Archangel Gabriel
The single eye means that we should envision *only good*.

------------------------------------------------------

*Bible*
*There is no fear in love; but perfect love casteth out fear; because fear hath torment. He that feareth is not made perfect in love.* I John 4:18

*Archangel Gabriel*
You don't *have* perfect love, health, mind; you *are* those things.

*Author*
Our task is to apply our perfect love to pure thoughts, words and deeds. It is not difficult when we ask the Holy Spirit to guide us - constantly. He will respond, unfailingly.

------------------------------------------------------

In this seminar, Gabriel told us that the Lord's Prayer "is the affirming of all you require on earth; to make you aware." He then explained it:

*Our Father* – Creator
*Who art in Heaven* – perfection
*Holy is Your name* – unification of parent and child
*Thy kingdom* – of spirit; all kingdoms
*Come* - to this earth as in Heaven
*Give us this day* – awaken your awareness to the Spirit of You in your Oneness of God

*Our daily bread* – true bread\*
*Forgive us* – as long as we believe we need to be
*Lead us* – to the light of awareness that we have never sinned
*The power* – God is the only power

Pray with the knowingness of your connectedness to God. Do *not* use God's name to curse. The purpose of prayer is to know God, and the purpose of meditation is to know God knows you.

*In another prayer given us by Gabriel (a female version of the 23rd Psalm), true bread is 'Thy Presence in my consciousness'. See Introduction.

---------------------------------------------------------------------------

Prayer and Meditation 11/23/91
*Bible*
*Pray without ceasing.* I Th. 5:17

*Archangel Gabriel*
Be aware of you as a living prayer. Your very existence is a form of prayer. The prayer is you.

*Author*
When we see ourselves as a living prayer, then to 'pray without ceasing' means we ought to be always aware that in our daily lives as we move through our days we constitute prayer - a worshipful acknowledgment that we are God's Own. This is not a difficult task when we consciously seek guidance from the Holy Spirit. But we must seek it. The Holy Spirit will guide us always, and unfailingly, when we request His help --- in the workplace, at home doing everything, and (of course) in our prayers and meditations.

# CHAPTER FOUR

# 1992

5/23/92 Sacred Thread
*Bible*
*Thus the heavens and the earth were finished, and all the host of them. And on the seventh day God ended his work which he has made; and he rested on the seventh day from all his work which he had made.* Gen. 2:1-2

*Author*
These seven days represent the \*Seven Rays of vibration that bring formlessness to form. We developed other rays; 'each thread a type of consciousness'. Gabriel said we also created universes! (Reader please note the plural is not a typo). Our creative mind never creates negatives, for it is holy; it is sacred.

Author note: The seven Rays are described in detail in Gabriel's seminars entitled *The Seven Rays,* given 4/8/89 and 4/15/89. These seminars are not included here, as Gabriel did not quote scripture therein.

-----------------------------------------------------------------------

*Bible*
*The light of the body is the eye: if therefore thine eye be single, thy whole body shall be full of light.* Matt. 6:22

*Archangel Gabriel*
It means if you focus only on spiritual things your whole body will be spiritual. 'eye be single' does not mean to review sins and continue self-punishment – that is a wedge between you and God."
When Gabriel says 'the whole body will be spiritual' means that we will be guided by the Holy Spirit in all aspects of our life - all aspects

-----------------------------------------------------------------------

7/25/92 The Sacred Garden

*Bible*
*And he said unto them, Take nothing for your journey, neither staves, nor scrip, neither bread, neither money; neither have two coats apiece.* Luke 9:3

*Archangel Gabriel:*
Jesus told the apostles 'don't take shoes, extra coat' because things are not representative of abundance. The feeling of lack is from your soul's memory; from the ego: a sense of separation of you from God. What you give with love will come back to you. It is a spiritual law.

--------------------------------------------------------------------------

*Bible*
*There came unto him a woman having an alabaster box of very precious ointment, and poured it on his head, as he sat at meat.* Matt. 26:7

*Archangel Gabriel:*
Jesus said, *'You have the poor with you always.' Matt. 26:11* There are some who always remain in a state of need because they are not aware of the God within Helping the poor with money is no help. Helping the poor is talking to them; to teach awareness of who they are; give [them] tools to work with.

*Author*
All the apostles wrote about the woman who poured expensive oil on Jesus' head. The response of the apostles was criticism, for they said the ointment could have been sold and the money given to the poor.

--------------------------------------------------------------------------

*Archangel Gabriel*
Mohammed, Buddha, Jesus – none proclaimed they were the *only* messengers of God – all were one. Scripture is a history of people's ideas of what happens to a person. 'thou shalt not's' are limiting, hindering, inhibiting. Most of you feel guilty when having a good time, [believing you] offend a wrathful god. God is not aware of anything he did not create.

*Author*

The Good Book says 'honor thy father and mother and in their old age cast them not out'." (All of the synoptic gospels mention this). Parents help their children always; never say 'no'. How many think your children will be there for YOU as you were there for them?" (Author note: no hands went up)

--------------------------------------------------------------------------------

9/26/92 Building Spiritual Power
*Archangel Gabriel (on the crucifixion)*
John was the only one who understood the secrets of the universe; the only one who completely trusted Jesus; the only one who absolutely believed in Jesus' power, though he did not understand it. Only John believed in miracles... Seeing Jesus on the cross, he [John] was torn between the divinity of Jesus and the agony from his five senses. He beat on a brick wall until he bled. His spirit told him to pray and look at the cross. He saw a light; a truth winged and free.

He said 'What is it?'

Jesus appeared to him and said, 'You are seeing truth. I am not in pain. The multitudes see *their illusion* of hatred and death. There is no death or hatred; only love'.

At the tomb Peter went in, but John knew, because he had gone beyond the reasoning mind; was able to transcend limitations.

You are on a sacred journey; a holy quest - not to find your center, but to allow your consciousness to take in the power of the Holy Spirit and let it flow through you. Then the physical form is transformed by it and you are healed.

[Regarding one's own 'death' experience, Gabriel told us that John consciously chose his physical passing]: John bid men to dig a grave. He disrobed and said, 'I am going to the spirit world', laid in the grave and died. This is doable by you.

-------------------------------------------------------------------

11/21/92 Gifts of the Spirit
*Archangel Gabriel*
You once knew all levels of consciousness. You communicated with angels, nature, unseen things. You instantly knew all answers. You didn't have to learn anything. I am your reminder.

-------------------------------------------------------------------

*Bible*
*Resist not evil.* Matt.5:39

*Archangel Gabriel*
This means let the negative go by and do not engage it. Never argue with ego. When negative presents itself, center yourself, picture a beam of light within.

# CHAPTER FIVE

# 1993

3/27/93 Holy Breath of Life
*Bible*
*And God said, Let there be light. And there was light.* Gen. 1:3

*Archangel Gabriel*
This light was the divine Will of God, Gabriel said. It is not an outward, going from force, but a becoming; expressing life. This becomingness is in three stages:

First, the positive force - male energy - causes changes which you perceive every day as sequential. It would appear to divide itself, and you call this 'space'.

Second, as you focus your love toward others, they grow from that love. The becoming must know It's Source: Divine Love.

Third, you must *experience* divine love. The Holy Spirit is divine love in action. Christ love, Christ consciousness, is spiritual truth. It is not religious. If you were not a Christian group I would use another term.

------------------------------------------------------------------------

*Bible*
*But he said unto them, I have meat to eat that ye know not of."* John 5:39

*Archangel Gabriel:*
You can tune to mother earth: lay down on her face and feel her, and feed your body without food. Breath in energy and feed the form of the Temple of God. Your cells must become healthy; unhealthy cells go from the body.

## 6/19/93 Breaking Resistance Barriers

*Bible*
*And he was withdrawn from them about a stones cast, and kneeled down and prayed, Saying, Father, if thou be willing, remove this cup from me: nevertheless not my will, but thine, be done. And there appeared an angel unto him from heaven, strengthening him. And being in an agony he prayed more earnestly:* and his sweat was as it *were* great drops of blood falling down to the ground. Luke 22:41-44.

*Archangel Gabriel*
At Gethsemane Jesus lost sight of his Christness. He had to go past his pain and realize it was non-existent, and go forth in the fullness of his Godness. You are all on your crosses. You chose to come off this day*, and it is why you are here. To take you out of the crucifixion, and to your resurrection.

*Author note: All Gabriel' lessons are directed to all humankind.

*Author*
We need to affirm I AM whenever we are tempted to see ourselves as less than what we are. We are more than anything that appears to us. We need to add one word after I AM: love. It is essential to watch what we say after I AM, for it is an affirmation of our true, sacred selves. Each I AM breaks the wall of resistance. "You grandly love your limitations," Gabriel said. Real courage is gentle, internal, God awareness. Perfect love disallows negative energy forever.

-------------------------------------------------------------------------

## 7/24/93 Chambers of the Heart
*Bible*
*Thou shalt not kill. Thou shalt not commit adultery. Thou shalt not. Thou shalt not steal. Thou shalt not bear false witness against thy neighbour. Thou shalt not covet thy neighbour's house; thou shalt not covet thy neighbour's wife, nor his manservant, nor his maidservant, nor his ox, nor his ass, nor anything that is thy neighbour's. Ex. 20: 13-17*

*Archangel Gabriel*
These 'Thou shalt not's' are totally useless in your journey home to God, for it is a limitation impossible to keep - but spirit is limitless.

When you feel held in a vise of limitations that is when your pain (of feeling distant from God) is greatest. Your limits are time (clocks, schedules), distance, space [mine and yours], nationality, race, color. Dividing yourselves up constantly in separation, you brought into form your belief in the separation from God, Which is unconditional, unspeakable Love.

-----------------------------------------------------------------------

*Bible*
*But I say unto you, Love your enemies, bless them that curse you, do good to them that hate you, and pray for them which despitefully use you, and persecute you; Matt. 5: 44; Luke 6: 27*

*Archangel Gabriel*
Conflicting with others creates blockages on your spiritual path back home to God. To prevent, or face conflict, you need to accept yourselves as children of God, accept others as children of God, and know that you, and they, in your sacredness, have the right to be who you are.

[In this seminar Gabriel explained the meaning of the Lord's Prayer (female version). He said the words would open the chambers of our hearts to the extent we are willing them to be open. We must invite the Holy Spirit into the chambers of our hearts.]

<u>*The Lord's Prayer (female version):*</u>

*Our Mother* - the nurturing aspect of God.

*Who art the sacred space within* - where you come to know God; sacred silence - not without sound, but all sound (as white is all colors) - harmonized and allowed to be.

*Holy is thy name* - Could it be anything else?

*Thy Kingdom be manifested in all levels of my being, as it is manifested in the sacred space of my Spirit Self.*

Could there be anything more accepting of you? When we come to recognize that manifestation is necessary on all levels, then we are consciously aware of the divinity within at all times.

*Cause me this day to be aware of the bread of life: thy presence in my consciousness.* The bread of life is the substance of everything we are; it radiates livingness.

*Help me to release all error perceptions of myself and others* - when you are willing to release and let go of your limitations, they will fall away.

*Keep me aware of Thee, my Source, for then shall I be delivered from the illusion of separateness* - keep a concrete awareness of God within.

*For Thine is the Kingdom of my being, the Glory of my light, and the Power of my spirit; now and forever.* Amen

Then you KNOW the Kingdom to be part of you. What but God is the Glory and the Power of You?

You can use this prayer, and internalize the explanation, or you wouldn't be here.

It is very helpful to picture within a brilliant light, representing the Light of God, which is brighter than a thousand suns.

---------------------------------------------------------------------------

10/1-10/3/93 Making Spirit Life Real

This was one of the few weekend retreats by Archangel Gabriel. They were wonderful. We gathered on a Friday evening, at a reserved location where housing was available. It was a time of rest and relaxation at the end of our busy weeks, as we all had occupations and families. Saturday Gabriel spoke to us all morning, and in the afternoon. We took about an hour for lunch and two short breaks. Sunday morning Gabriel gave a short message, and the weekend came to an end with his closing prayer.

The Garden of Eden is described in Genesis, Chapter 2.

*Archangel Gabriel*
The Garden of Eden is your spirit Self. Adam (action) and Eve (sustaining energy) are aspects of all. The spirit of you is innocent, loving, beautiful, and joyous.

--------------------------------------------------------------------

*Bible*
*But of the tree of the knowledge of good and evil thou shalt not eat of it: for in the day that thou eatest thereof thou shalt surely die. Gen. 2:17*

*Archangel Gabriel*
The tree in the garden represents your endless possibilities.

--------------------------------------------------------------------

*Bible*
*And the Lord God called unto Adam, and said unto him, where art thou? And he said, I heard thy voice in the garden, and I was afraid, because I was naked; and I hid myself. And he said, who told you that you were naked?* Gen. 3:9-11

*Archangel Gabriel*
This is the most important part of scripture. 'Who told you, [Gabriel to audience], 'that you must cover up your glory and your power?'

You still feel unsafe in your nakedness (error perceptions) and you still have a blaming attitude. You need to come to know who you really are.

--------------------------------------------------------------------

*Bible*
*For now we see through a glass, darkly; but then face to face: now I know in part; but then shall I know even as also I am known.* I Cor. 13:12

*Archangel Gabriel*
It is time to realize that you have come home.

*Author*
When we listen to the Voice of God and respond to it, we shall know the God within ourselves and the God within others. Inside all life is a spark of divinity - forever undisturbed or unmarred.

11/20/93 Beginning Ascension 101
*Bible*
*Humble yourselves in the sight of the Lord, and he shall lift you up.* James 4:10

*For it is written, as I live, saith the Lord, every knee shall bow to me, and every tongue shall confess to God.* Rom 14:11

*Archangel Gabriel*
Everyone shall bow before Divine Essence, not fear. Then you shall be lifted up into your awareness of your at-one-ment with God.

*Author*
When I heard this seminar title I was expecting some holy guidance about how to take my body up to God, as Jesus did, when he ascended. What a surprise to hear Gabriel talk about our daily life, our food, and how we feel about our bodies! But, as he explained, we must learn to love and care for our bodies, or else why would we want to take them with us!

# CHAPTER SIX

# 1994

1/15/94 Polarizing energies
*Bible*
*There were giants in the earth in those days; and also after that, when the sons of God came in unto the daughters of men, and they bare children to them, the same became mighty men which were of old, men of renown.* Gen. 6:4

*Archangel Gabriel*
These giants were you; from Atlantis; with large heads and small bodies. Atlantians performed scientific experiments on others; your hearts became very small. You created constantly until you developed a huge head, with a small body - not much love was expressed. When a race abandons love it leads to destruction, for love is the foundation of life. Mating with females on Earth, offspring became more loving.

-----------------------------------------------------------------------------

*Bible*
*But I say unto you, Love your enemies, bless them that curse you, do good to them that hate you, and pray for them which despitefully use you, and persecute you.* Matt. 5:44

*Archangel Gabriel*
You did not hear it. Love is the opposite of hate. Fear leads to hate and repeats.

-----------------------------------------------------------------------------

*Bible*
*And he said unto them, Ye will surely say unto me this proverb, Physician, heal thyself: whatsoever we have heard done in Capernaum, do also here in*

*thy country. And he said, Verily I say unto you, No prophet is accepted in his own country.* Luke 4:23-24

*Archangel Gabriel*
You need to get your lives in order. Change your busy-ness to constructive forms. Get your lives in order. This means waking up in the morning and having nothing to dread; to go to bed at night not frustrated about the day. It means not having a feeling of stagnation, of emptiness, of 'nothing to do'. Be adventurous; it is an opportunity to solve. Anticipate wondrous results and profound love, and a sense of well-being. This is self-healing, and leads to healing others by your example.

In the early 1900s [there was a] Theory of Evolution - that you were from the monkeys. The head monkey asked for an audience with God and told God they were very upset with such an idea!

All your unhappy situations can be changed by you, for you were created from love and joy.

--------------------------------------------------------------------------

9/17/94 Effective Use of Spiritual Tools I
*Bible*
*For I will shew him how great things he must suffer for my name's sake.* Acts 9:16

*Archangel Gabriel:*
The old-time religion speaks of suffering. Did you come here [Earth] to swear, get mad, feel pain, have conflicts with another? You did not come here for these reasons. You came to learn without suffering. You came here to be in peace, harmony, love, joy. Jesus did not come to pay the debts of others. He, and Buddha, and others, came to show you how to live from the spirit of you.

--------------------------------------------------------------------------

10/8/94 Effective Use of Spiritual Tools II
*Bible*
*And God said, Let there be light; and there was light.* Gen. 1:3

*Archangel Gabriel:*
Light is what you are made of. There are two great lights - the sun and the moon. I'll speak of son (sun): S stands for spirit, O stands for oneness (union with God), and N is 'naturally'. You chose darkness; God did not. In the darkness you perceived that you 'could not know', and developed your five senses in a form (body) that you could feel safe in. But there is no safety in ignorance. It makes you vulnerable to all non-truths and superstitions.

---

11/12/94 Effective Use of Spiritual Tools III
*Bible*
*But the ship was now in the midst of the sea, tossed with waves: for the wind was contrary. And in the fourth watch of the night Jesus went unto them, walking on the sea. And when the disciples saw him walking on the sea, they were troubled, saying, it is a spirit; and they cried out of fear. But straightway Jesus spake unto them, saying, be of good cheer; it is I; be not afraid.* Matt. 14:24-27

*Archangel Gabriel*
The New Testament has a thousand stories. They are all yours. For 5,000 years you have placed before you repeatedly the same stories, myths, allegories to teach you. And here you are. 'Come to me, God says'. It is time to do it.

*Author*
It is time to wake up to the truth of us - that we are light beings, children of the Living God, able to overcome every problem on our path because we put it there. Gabriel said we can - and must - control our lives; even our weather! At another seminar Gabriel instructed us to join him in controlling the weather. He did this when several attendees were travelling back home to New York City and New Jersey, and stormy weather was predicted. By unanimous consent, we envisioned fifty degrees and no precipitation. The weather was exactly that - on that day *and* the next four days! This is something we can all do; at any time we desire good weather - for driving, golfing, sailing or any other activity. Not to seek an 80 degree day in December, but within reason to plan the weather to suit our day.

# CHAPTER SEVEN

# 1995

3/13/95 Question and answer session by Archangel Gabriel

In compiling this book of Gabriel's lessons I did not, for the most part, review the Q and A periods of his lessons. Often the questioner went off the topic and asked irrelevant questions. However, in March of 1995 Gabriel specifically identified the meaning of 'the fires of hell', saying that it means 'the fires of anger; there is no hell'. Elsewhere in his teachings Gabriel told us that the original meaning of 'hell' was 'a shallow grave'. As such, it was an ominous threat, because to have one's bones dug up was a permeating fear. I suspect this leads to inquiry into myth, which is outside the scope of this writing. But Gabriel did tell us to 'read your mythology.'

One might ask why, then, do we find 'hell' in scripture; both in the Old Testament and the New Testament. Thousands of years ago the belief in hell was all-pervasive. Jesus spoke of 'hell' because although he knew it did not exist, he also knew the people still accepted it as their truth.

---------------------------------------------------------------

3/18/95 Windows of the Mind
*Bible*
*And they stripped him, and put on him a scarlet robe. And when they had platted a crown of thorns, they put it upon his head, and a reed in his right hand: and they* bowed *the knee before him, and mocked him, saying, Hail, King of the Jews! And they spit upon him, and took the reed, and smote him on the head.* Matt. 27:28-30

*Archangel Gabriel*
Anger is a reaction of the emotional body saying you have the right to 'get even with', to 'teach a lesson to', etc. If you get angry, don't do anything

with it. Confirm the all-encompassing love of your feeling nature, and no anger comes."

*Author*

When Jesus was stripped he showed no anger. When a crown of thorns was placed on Jesus' head he did not get angry. When the soldiers spit upon him, he did not get angry. He did not get angry because he knew what we have yet to learn: anger never straightens out anything; anger is never justified. Beyond the bodies and the behaviors Jesus saw the spark of divinity within his persecutors, and prayed to the Father for their awareness of it.

-----------------------------------------------------------------------

*Bible*

*Therefore take no thought, saying, what shall we eat? Or, What shall we drink? Or, Wherewithal shall we be clothed? (For all these things do the Gentiles seek:) for your heavenly Father knoweth that ye have need of all these things. But seek ye first the kingdom of God, and his righteousness; and all these things shall be added unto you.* Matt. 6:31-33

*Fear not, little flock; for it is your Father's good pleasure to give you the kingdom.* Luke 12:32

*Archangel Gabriel*

What you are supposed to have, you will want.

*Author*

We need to know that we are worth what we ask for. If we were not meant to have it we would not want it. It is interesting to note that Luke calls the people 'little flock'. It is a direct reference to Jesus' position as our shepherd (John, Chapter 10), and thus we are his sheep. But unlike sheep, once we follow his precepts, we must voluntarily ask for his guidance, and then follow it on our own. As his spiritual siblings we can easily follow his example, if we choose. When we seek only our highest good, we can have everything else.

-----------------------------------------------------------------------

*Bible*
*Verily, verily, I say unto you, He that believeth on me, the works that I do shall he do also; and greater works than these shall he do; because I go unto my Father.* John 14:12

*Archangel Gabriel*
Every spiritual truth comes as a blessing. When you don't see the blessing, it will hit you over the head.

*Author*
How often we receive a blessing but do not see it as such until years later. Other times we fail to see a blessing, and then another identifies it immediately for us, and it hits us like a bolt. Even the things we think people 'did to us' become lessons in truth and we acknowledge them as blessings. I do not know what 'greater things' we could do than Jesus did, but perhaps he meant that in this Age of Truth more people will be open to living a life of love and forgiveness. And then we can become examples to follow, as we follow Jesus' example.

-------------------------------------------------------------------------

5/20/95 Five Gates of Initiation
*Bible*
*In the beginning was the Word, and the Word was with God, and the Word was God.* John 1:1

*Archangel Gabriel*
The Word is the Christ in you.

*Author*
At another time - I think it was a Q and A session - Gabriel asked us each to say I AM, give our name, followed by 'the Christ'.
When it came my turn, I said, 'I am Ellen the Christ'. It sounded foreign to me. I don't know how others felt. It still sounds foreign to me, twenty years later. Yet I know it is true, because my teacher, Gabriel, said so. He also said we are slow learners. We have the power to uncreate all of our situations; all our pain. The way to do it is forgive - everyone, for everything.

---

*Bible*
*And I, if I be lifted up from the earth, will draw all men unto me.* John 12:32

*Archangel Gabriel:*
The Christ in him… will draw up all the personality, feelings, ideas that you created, and bring you home. But you must first be consciously aware of your connectedness to the spirit of you.

*Author*
The ascension of us all; each of us, will come about when we have this conscious awareness, and not before.

---

*Bible*
*Jesus sayeth unto him, Thomas, because thou hast seen me, thou hast believed: blessed are they that have not seen, and yet have believed.* John 20:29

*Archangel Gabriel*
[when you 'die'] You leave trails of light, as a comet, for souls who come to earth after you; as you followed others.

*Author*
What a beautiful thought this is. Trails of light invisible to our physical eyes, guide the spirit of us, and draw us to it; unseen but not unknown. We can apply this idea to our firm conviction of following Jesus' path back home.

---

7/15/95 Beside the Still Waters
*Bible*
*Ye shall seek me, and shall not find me: and where I am, thither ye cannot come.* John 7:34

*Archangel Gabriel*

Each person has their own place in the stillness, into which no other can come. All humanity is 'the only begotten' Son of God. But in that at-one-ment you each have our your own spiritual path back home to God, based on your personal choices and experiences. You have become unaware of it, and your awakening to it will take you back home.

------------------------------------------------------------------------

*Bible*

*Enter ye in at the strait gate: for wide is the gate, and broad is the way, that leadeth to destruction, and many there be which go in thereat: Because straight is the gate, and narrow is the way, which leadeth unto life, and few there be that find it. Beware of false prophets, which come to you in sheep's clothing, but inwardly they are ravening wolves.* Matt. 7:13-15

*My sheep hear my voice, and I know them, and they follow me: And I give unto them eternal life; and they shall never perish, neither shall any man pluck the out of my hand* John 10:27-28

*Archangel Gabriel*

The gate is the entrance to the silence (today's lesson). 'know my voice' is the Voice of God within. The 'wolves in sheep's clothing' is your error perception that you and God will never meet. It is an error perception that you are unloved, unwanted, unworthy. Jesus did not seek to find the Christ; he did seek to *be* the Christ. You are here to bring light - so let it come in.

------------------------------------------------------------------------

*Bible*

*Jesus saith unto him, I am the way, the truth, and the life: no man cometh unto the Father, but by me.* John 14:6

*Archangel Gabriel*

Jesus said this not as a Christian - he was a Jew. He said 'I am one of you; do what I have done and be what I am, for what I am you are, and I have discovered myself, but you have not discovered yourself'.

------------------------------------------------------------

*Bible*
*The Lord is my shepherd; I shall not want. He maketh me to lie down in green pastures: he leadeth me beside the still waters.* Psalm 23:1-2

*Archangel Gabriel*
Gabriel explained the stillness:

The stillness restores the connection to your soul and spirit.

The stillness restores the experience you long since forgot.

The stillness opens you to be aware of what is contained in your soul and the very gnosis of your spirit.

The limitlessness of the stillness allows you to learn and *know* mysteries the world knows not (such as the universes); to know the vastness of other realms outside the earth.

In the stillness you receive. You are not rejecting anything, you are not judging, you are not projecting. The stillness transcends all limits - out of the ego's clutches. It frees you to enter into the truth and know it, understand it, be it. It allows you to be the truth of you. It brings you to a knowingness where nothing bothers you, and you know illusion when you see it - once you have seen real spirit. Nothing of earth can tie you down or beleaguer you. Go forth and be the master you have chosen to be, without any Achilles heel. The soul is the recorder of the past; the spirit is the past, present, and future.

------------------------------------------------------------

9/16/95 Opening of the Internal Door
*Bible*
*And his fame went out throughout all Syria: and they brought unto him all sick people that were taken with divers diseases and torments, and those which were possessed with devils, and those which were lunatick, and those that had the palsy; and he healed them.* Matt. 4:24

*Archangel Gabriel*

Jesus could heal because he knew and lived the truths I bring you every time I come. What he knew, you can know. What he is, you are.

There must be a grounding force for love, or how will every truth we bring [to you] stay? Jesus came because the earth needed transforming. 2,000 years later it is still being transformed.

*Bible*

*Then they took away the stone from the place where the dead was laid. And Jesus lifted up his eyes, and said, Father, I thank thee that thou hast heard me. And I knew that thou hearest me always: but because of the people which stand by I said it, that they may believe that thou hast sent me. And when he thus had spoken, he cried with a loud voice, Lazarus, come forth.* John 11:41-43

*Archangel Gabriel*

When Jesus raised Lazarus from the tomb, he knew the truth - that there is no death, that he was the Son of God, and that he could bring forth life.

*Author*

The world consciousness is much the same now as it was then. For at the mourners at Lazarus' tomb, we also would have joined in the perception of death, and the tomb it represented. Jesus knew the crowd perceived a make-believe world of their own creation. We still do. Truth was brought by Gabriel and eleven master teachers simultaneously, in this dawning of this Age of Truth. We must awaken to the light within each of us. It is what the Bible tells us: the Kingdom of God is within. *Now* is the time to accept and live our truth. We must seek perception of truth in place of our error perceptions. We are children of God. God, our spiritual parent, patiently awaits our return.

-------------------------------------------------------------------------

*Bible*

*And if any mischief follow, then thou shalt give life for life, Eye for eye, tooth for tooth, hand for hand, foot for foot, Burning for burning, wound for wound.* Ex. 23-25; Lev. 24:20

*Archangel Gabriel*

It is the personality of you which believes in 'eye for eye; tooth for tooth', and manifests what you believe. The personality has not let itself be redeemed by the Christ. It keeps the old concept of cause and effect, and so it created karma. Whatever you think can happen, you become a channel for it to happen to you, because you open the possibility of it, and manifest what you believe.

*Author*

With this information from Gabriel, we can see that all we receive we make happen ourselves. On the one hand it demonstrates our power. On the other hand it demonstrates what a low opinion we have of self - to create all the problems we encounter in life, and all the failed relationships. We will be free of the karmic ties only when we let ourselves be redeemed by the Christ, by placing the ego in a proper perspective and allowing Love (God) to be our Guide. As long as we continue to believe in this ancient precept of 'eye for eye' we will continue to harbor resentments, seek revenge, and engage in wars. How many more centuries will we fail to embrace love as our guiding light, and discover our Selves?

-------------------------------------------------------------------------------

*Bible*

*Now the serpent was more subtil than any beast of the field which the Lord had made. And he said unto the woman, Yea, hath God said, Ye shall not eat of every tree of the garden? Gen. 3:1*

*Archangel Gabriel*

The serpent was the perception which says 'present a certain appearance to the world' - i.e., you would not wear pajamas to a business meeting. You believe you must present a certain face to the world. It never occurs to you that you can present yourself as you, child of God: your honest, loving, truthful, wise self.

*Author*

Gabriel also said that it is only our perceptions that keep us from being happy. We must get past the perceptions. What are they? Whatever our five senses tell us. Instead, we can and must recognize the Voice of God within. It is soft, gentle, profound, and sweet. It says to us, 'You are loveable'.

-----------------------------------------------------------------------

*Bible*
*And I will bring the blind by a way that they knew not; I will lead them in paths that they have not known: I will make darkness light before them, and crooked things straight. These things will I do unto them, and not forsake them. Is 42:16*

*Archangel Gabriel*
Write your own script and you will know the reality (a great life) of the isness of you. You will then have no complications, no failure, no struggle, no despair. Say 'The Lord God of me goes ahead to make straight my path'.

*Author*
Sadly, we all listen to the ego, with all its fear-based warnings, like 'Better not', 'What if? 'You are not worthy', 'You're too old, too small, too poor'. God knows us as His children of light. He is the Father of lights (James 1:17). We all have a swamp on our path. We can choose to stay or change the swamp.

-----------------------------------------------------------------------

*Bible*
*And the Word was made flesh, and dwelt among us, (and we beheld his glory, the glory as of the only begotten of the Father, full of grace and truth.* John 1:14

*Archangel Gabriel*
It was in this lesson by Archangel Gabriel that he explained a significant error in translation of this biblical phrase. The original words were; 'the son, begotten of the only God'.

*Author*

What a difference this explanation gives! We all are His only begotten children! When we believe that Jesus is the only Son of God, it is impossible to emulate him. Keeping him suffering on the cross precludes our ability to emulate him. Yet he said 'follow me' many times in scripture. He said *For I have given you an example, that ye should do as I have done to you.* John 13:15

------------------------------------------------------------

*Bible*

*And he was there in the wilderness forty days, tempted of Satan; and was with the wild beasts; and the angels ministered unto him.* Mark 1:13

*Archangel Gabriel*

Archangel Gabriel said that there is no Satan; there is no hell. Humans invented both. The 'tempter' was Jesus' own ego. In this lesson Gabriel told a wonderful story about Jesus' experience in the wilderness: When Jesus sat by a fire at night, he found little creatures there. 'One night two big male lions came to the fire and regarded him (there was no fear of man then). They sensed exquisite peace, love, connectedness, and went close to bask in his presence, and laid by him at the fire. If he was in his perception he would have expressed fear; but he knew there was nothing mightier than he. He knew his spiritual truth was far more powerful than the lions… You all have your lions - you could fear, or know you are more'.

------------------------------------------------------------

*Bible*

*But be ye doers of the word, and not hearers only, deceiving your own selves.* James 1:22

*Archangel Gabriel*

Archangel Gabriel reminded us of this phrase in James, and said that we chose to be here (on Earth) to learn. The day's entire lesson 'offers you a way to learn and become doers of the Word'. He told us not to be afraid to call in the power of the Living Christ, by saying, 'Thank you, Father, that you hear me always'.

-------------------------------------------------------------------

11/18/95 Total Living
*Bible*
*And when Jesus had cried with a loud voice, he said, Father, into thy hands I commend my spirit: and having said thus, he gave up the ghost.* Luke 23:46

*Archangel Gabriel*
When you came to earth you asked for grace to accept all the experiences and all the people you chose, to carry you to this moment. Say [to the Father], 'Into Thy hands I commend the totality of my being'. You must be aware of the moment's blessings on you; not think of the past or future. The only time in eternity is 'now'. Basing your decisions on the past keeps you there. Projecting into the future is not valid because although time is linear, your spiritual path is not. It is vertical. It is uniquely your own. Awareness of the blessings of now takes you back home to God.

-------------------------------------------------------------------

*Bible*
*His lord said unto him, Well done, thou good and faithful servant: thou hast been faithful over a few things, I will make thee ruler over many things: enter thou into the joy of thy lord.* Matt. 25:21

*Archangel Gabriel*
You will fulfill the plans that you made before you came to earth. You will do so, in misery or joy, and hear, 'Well done, thou good and faithful servant'.

# CHAPTER EIGHT

# 1996

___

1/20/96 Taking the Next Step
*Bible*
*Verily, verily, I say unto you, He that believeth on me, the works that I do shall he do also; and greater works than these shall he do; because I go unto my Father.* John 14:12

*Therefore doth my Father love me, because I lay down my life, that I might take it again. No man taketh it from me, but I lay it down of myself. I have power to lay it down, and I have power to take it again. This commandment have I received of my Father.* John 10:17-18

*Archangel Gabriel*
The Master Jesus had a great lesson to learn. When he started on his path, he held fast to one idea, and he never let it go: 'The Kingdom of Heaven is within, and I can live and experience the Kingdom'.

Gabriel then showed us a side of Jesus we did not know:

But he had no patience with those who did not believe it. Jesus had a temper and as a young man, as he taught the scribes and Pharisees, he did not meet challenge very gracefully. He wondered, why can't they listen to me? At times he shook his fist in their faces, and his anger seemed attacking. They said, Isn't this the son of Mary?...

Joseph [Jesus' father] was a gentle, patient man, and had learned that you accomplish more with honey than vinegar. Joseph shows Jesus, by demonstration, how to set up a beehive to get honey. Then he says to Jesus, 'What would have happened if we put vinegar on the hive?'... Jesus learned then that you get far greater results with sweetness. Then Gabriel said to us, his students, You need to learn that which he was.

---

*Bible*
*Every knee shall bow.* Is. 45:23, Romans 14:11

*Archangel Gabriel*
Jesus left in a state of fulfillment, and he has come to complete the cycle. He has never left the earth; he is ever working to help others upward. 'Every knee shall bend' is not inequality, but complete harmony; completion.

---

*Bible*
*And he went a little farther, and fell on his face, and prayed, saying, O my Father, if it be possible, let this cup pass from me: nevertheless not as I will, but as thou wilt.* (Matt. 26:39, Mark 14:36, Luke 22:42)

*Archangel Gabriel*
When Jesus said, 'Thy will be done', he stayed in his Christ consciousness throughout the crucifixion.

*Author*
In another lesson, Gabriel explained that this is why Jesus did not suffer on the cross.

---

*Bible*
*Jesus sayeth unto her, Touch me not; for I am not yet ascended to my Father....* (John 20:17).

*Archangel Gabriel*
If someone had touched Jesus, it would have brought him back to the three-dimensional world. He needed to be in command of the fourth dimension. What he meant was, 'don't touch me because I haven't got a good handle on it (4th dimension) yet'.

------------------------------------------------------------------------

*Bible*
*Be not forgetful to entertain strangers: for thereby some have entertained angels unawares.* Heb. 13:2

Archangel Gabriel:
Yes, then too, angels appeared in many guises.

------------------------------------------------------------------------

3/11/96 Q and A session with Jesus the Christ

*Bible*
*Jesus saith unto him, I am the way, the truth, and the life: no man cometh unto the Father, but by me.* John 14:6

*Jesus the Christ*
[This means] that the Christ within must be known and felt, to go to the Father. Remember, I am with you always.

------------------------------------------------------------------------

Q. Please speak about the church councils and the apocryphal books

A. There were several councils, from broader to more rigid. Very selfish men left out all the apocryphal books.

------------------------------------------------------------------------

3/16/96 Winds of Change
*Bible*
*And I saw a new heaven and a new earth; for the first heaven and the first earth were passed away.* Rev.21:1

*Archangel Gabriel*
'A new heaven and a new earth' means a higher state of consciousness in humans of the earth. All this began 2,000 years ago, when it made

itself known to a handful of people. People then were rigid; now there is a freedom which was unheard of then. It [freedom] would have been considered sinful.

… You are all instruments of truth; a new wind is blowing. What I am about to say [today's lesson] will be misread, misunderstood. But as you go along your path, gradually you will find you are no longer thinking, but knowing.

---

*Bible*
*Therefore the Lord God sent him forth from the Garden of Eden, to till the ground from whence he was taken.* Gen 3:23

*Archangel Gabriel*
Nobody threw you out of the garden of Eden. It [Eden] was a state of consciousness where you communed with God; listened to the Voice of God. Adam obeyed. When God said, 'Do you love me?', Adam said, 'Of course'. Then you got so enthralled with distress, and nurtured it until it attracted much more, [until] you believed that it was impossible to walk in the garden with God. Sadness has no life except what you give it. Leave it behind; do not recall it to life and re-feed it.

---

*Bible*
*Whither shall I go from thy spirit? or whither shall I flee from thy presence? If I ascend up into heaven, thou art there: if I make my bed in hell, behold, thou art there. If I take the wings of the morning, and dwell in the uttermost parts of the sea; even there shall thy hand lead me, and thy right hand shall hold me.* Psalm 139:7-10

*Archangel Gabriel*
It is impossible to be where God is not. Yet you believe you are separate from God. We (angels) ever listen and hear the Voice say, 'I am the beginning and the end; I am Light. I am Energy. I am the Love that nurtures you. I am all things to all people all the time. I am the sun

and the moon. I am the breath you breathe. I am all that you are. There is no part of you that is not part of me'. When you 'left God' (in your consciousness), God said to us [angels] 'bring them back home'.

--------------------------------------------------------------------------

*Bible*
*Only with thine eyes shalt thou behold and see the reward of the wicked.*
Psalm 91:8

*Archangel Gabriel*
This should read '… reward of the ego'.

*Author*
Of course in the time this psalm was written, there was no such word as 'ego'. But, like all the other information Gabriel gave us regarding the Bible's symbolism, this clarification is logical. It makes sense to our 21st century minds.

--------------------------------------------------------------------------

5/18/96 Internal Awareness (Jesus and Gabriel)

At some of his seminars, Archangel Gabriel said there was one to follow him, but did not name 'him'. When Master Jesus first came he was asked for his name. He said names are not important, but for the time we could call him 'The One'. Then he said we could call him Lucas. Many months later, his identity became quite clear, when he said, 'I am the Christ'. This was the first seminar that Master Jesus came to us, through Reverend Penny. These were his first words to us, in a soft, gentle voice:

*Jesus the Christ*
I am the one to follow, and I will be with you for a short time this day, and then Gabriel will come to teach. I come this day to bring to your attention the necessity, on your part, to release forever and ever your idea of who you are, concerning the Earth. You are on the Earth, but you are not *of* the Earth. Your journey is a sacred journey, and your only commitment is to be at one-ment with God. Without that commitment,

no part of your journey has meaning. All the things that you disturb your thoughts with are meaningless. There is no part of your life that is not holy, and [there is] no part of your being that is not love.… Brothers and sisters, I have known what you know, and I have walked where you walk, and I have known pain; I have known death, and I can tell you, they are not real. They are the shadows of the shadows that you created, and nothing more - nothing more.

-------------------------------------------------------------------

*Bible*
*And that he might reconcile both unto God in one body by the cross, having slain the enmity thereby (Eph. 2:16)*

*Archangel Gabriel:*
The Master put upon the cross all the guilt of humankind, before and forever. All the observers at the cross saw them die. Then he came [as you will] the risen Son of God. Stop nurturing your guilt - put it up for adoption

*Author*
Here is another example of Gabriel's humor. It is highly significant that Gabriel referred to Jesus as 'The Master'. In another lesson Gabriel told us that we [humankind] are greater than the angels. He explained why - angels have free choice only in the realm of good; they do not understand anything negative. Humans, on the other hand, were given by God free choice across the board. And oh, what negative choices we have foolishly made! But when we turn within once more, and return home to God's realm - our natural habitat - what joy will be ours! The angels will rejoice with us.

-------------------------------------------------------------------

9/21/96 Awakening the Master Within (Jesus and Gabriel)
[Jesus the Christ came again, in the morning, followed by Gabriel in the afternoon]

*Bible*
*Blessed are the pure in heart: for they shall see God.* Matt. 5:8

*Jesus the Christ:*
[This means] letting go of judgment, letting go of the voice of the ego, letting go of the idea that your brother is the enemy, letting go of the part of you that was created by the ego. The true Self of you is the God in you. The God in you does not see your perception of evil. The God in you never looks on another as lesser than you; there is no point in it, for all are holy; pure.

*Archangel Gabriel*
You think that the spirit of you is furthest away (of all bodies). The spirit of you knows and encompasses all the others, but does not get caught up in the mental, emotional or physical bodies. The spirit of you reaches down into the rest of you. The spirit of you, expressing in you, is your consciousness. The mental body filters spirit into compartments created by past experiences. Your soul is the memory of you - the part which can know God and still be aware of your emotional, mental and spirit self.

*Author*
For a more detailed definition of our soul, read *Getting to Know Your Soul*, Gabriel's lessons by Rev Penny Donovan, published by iUniverse, 2004.

# CHAPTER NINE

# 1997

1/18/97 Master Jesus

In this seminar Gabriel gives us the 'back story' of Jesus' life and some of his past lives. He defines for us the Christ Consciousness. Gabriel also explains our devolution journey down into matter, which is beyond the scope of this writing. It is hoped the reader will read/hear all of Gabriel's lessons, preserved for future generations. See Audiology.

-------------------------------------------------------------------

*Bible*
*And lo a voice from heaven, saying, This is my beloved Son, in whom I am well pleased.* Matt. 3:17 (also in Mark and Luke)

*Archangel Gabriel*
You have a concept of love, but the love that is the Christ Consciousness is beyond your understanding. The ideal Son of God is all humans, without exception. The saint and the murderer are seen with the same eyes of love (I am not condoning murder) by the Christ. It encompasses all life: human, plant, animal, deva, mineral; all are a complete form of love. The closest on earth is a mother's love for her child, but it is beyond that. God looked upon Christ Consciousness and said, 'This is My beloved son, in whom I am well pleased'.

In regard to the book of Genesis, Gabriel said

There was no man named Adam; it is a state of consciousness. The Eden story came about in a male-dominated society. The female could produce; the male couldn't. The female had monthly power; the male feared her, so he put her in a subservient position to the male.

Regarding Jesus' past lives, Gabriel said he had many, as all humans do. But the archangel told us only of the ones in which Jesus had a shift in consciousness. In his other lifetimes Jesus, of course, had other names. Here is a recap of Jesus' previous incarnations as described by Gabriel:

*Enoch*
Enoch sought to find a connectedness to God. Part of you believes that you are connected to God.

*Hermes*
An alchemist who could transform anything into gold. The mythical Ra, in Egypt, believed he was God. It was the first time on earth that the idea of one God [Sun God] manifested. But Ra could not make rain or make the sun rise. Hermes affiliated with Ra to help Ra with his power. But Ra 'became so enthralled with himself that Hermes finally saw it was a lost cause, and withdrew'.

*Melchisedec*
*As he saith also in another place, Thou art a priest for ever after the order of Melchisedec.* Heb. 5:6 (also in Heb. Chapters 6 and 7)

Melchisedec is the first of Jesus' lifetimes which appears in scripture.
*And Abraham stretched forth his hand, and took the knife to slay his son.* Gen. 22:10

Melchisedec knew Abraham when he was Abram. He knew the consciousness of Abram, but he could not reach it. Abram had faith in the unseen; Melchisedec had *knowledge* of the unseen.

Communion explained
*And as they were eating, Jesus took bread, and blessed it, and brake it, and gave it to the disciples, and said, Take, eat; this is my body.* Matt. 26:26

Gabriel explained that back then people's minds were 'dull'. They believed in sacrifice (Abraham was ready to sacrifice his own son). You don't obliterate ignorance by slaying a lamb; external is not the answer; internal is needed.

The bread and wine [of Holy Communion] represented the internal connectedness to God. It is already within, but people [had to know] they were *doing* something [external]. Thus, Melchisedec gave Holy Communion to Abraham, and Abraham gave it to the people. Jesus saw Communion as a way to 'get it into the head' about the internal ness of life (spiritual). Bread was the staff of life to nomads - it could be made anywhere and it traveled without spoiling. The wine had to be the finest. Melchisedec lifted up the consciousness of man, by bringing external to internal. Melchisedec got his own awareness, too. We teach what we need to learn.

## Joseph
*Now Israel loved Joseph more than all his children, because he was the son of his old age: and he made him a coat of many colours.* Gen. 37:3

Joseph, whose father (Israel) gave him a coat of many colors, was Jesus' next lifetime. "[Israel] recognized in Joseph all states of consciousness". Joseph's brothers were jealous of him and decided to sell him to Egyptians traveling through, for thirty pieces of silver. "Sound familiar?" Gabriel said. For those unfamiliar with the Bible, Gabriel was referring to the thirty pieces of silver which Judas was paid by the Romans to betray Jesus. There is a long story about Joseph and his adventures in Egypt, which can be found in Genesis, chapters 37-43. At the end of the story Joseph forgives his brothers.

## Archangel Gabriel
Here is the first consciousness that you could live it [forgiveness]… Joseph saw his brothers with eyes of love; so much so, that he left the room to hide his tears.

## Joshua
There are 24 chapters in the Book of Joshua.

Archangel Gabriel tells us about Joshua's life, which I paraphrase here to save space. Moses knew what he had to do, to get to the Promised Land, but was afraid of angering God. So he said to Joshua (who had a warrior mentality), Can you help me? Moses represents law; unforgiving law (stone tablets). Moses also had a speech impediment, so he asked

Aaron to speak for him. On their way to the Promised Land, Joshua and the Israelites came to the Jordan River.

Jesus recalled that Moses separated the Red Sea. So he 'read' the signs of Earth and noticed earth tremors, indicating an earthquake was imminent. He ordered all the people to the river's edge, and an angel said, 'You've got the Ark of the Covenant, use it.' And so he ordered the carriers to take the Covenant into the water, which they did, fearing they might drown in doing so. The earthquake about 10 miles upstream stopped the flow of water, and they were free to cross.

Joshua knew that the Romans had chariots with wheels and spokes that could chop them to pieces. But he knew also they could not take the chariots up into the hills. And he had many men, so he took the battle to his own territory. Attacking all the cities, he finally came to Jericho. Jericho had never been taken; her people thought she was invincible. But Joshua new the walls were very old. He remembered, from Hermes, the power of vibration. So he got the people to march around, blowing horns for seven days. He told them, 'When I say 'blow horn' shout a mighty praise to God'. Joshua took off his shoes and walked barefoot so he could feel when the earthquake came. When it did, he gave the signal and the people shouted and blew horns, and the walls fell, Joshua commanded 'Take no prisoners', and all men, women and children were slaughtered.

*Archangel Gabriel:* Joseph was the forgiver; Joshua slaughtered. Joshua's actions represent an example of the misuse of our God-given power. As Joseph, he desired to bring his loving-kindness to our consciousness, but he did not. So he had to rid the human consciousness of limitation, in order to get to the Promised Land (Christ Consciousness). Christ Consciousness has nothing to do with Christians; Christ Consciousness is for all people.

## Buddha
Archangel Gabriel: Buddha was the Christ Consciousness for all forms of consciousness; for all on Earth.

Gabriel told about Buddha's life, recapped here: As son of a Rajah in India, Buddha lived a wealthy, protected life until he was thirty. He decided to travel outside the temple, and for the first time saw death, disease, poverty, hunger, decayed bodies. He did not understand how it could be. Instead of returning to his 'ivory tower', he left his wife and children, and began a quest to learn. He rejected all comforts, put on old rags for clothing and stopped eating, "until his intestines were nearly destroyed," Gabriel said.

He found no answers from the outside world, so he 'went within', by meditating in silence. When others saw him, they thought he was a guru, so they fed him and listened to him.

*Archangel Gabriel*: Buddha learned one great truth: that compassion, respect, love for *all life* was the only way to leave behind one's karma; [and] not to build any [more] by negative thinking.

There were two thoughts then: The Vedas (the law), and the Upanishads, which addressed the internal ness of God ('do not unto others what you would not have done to you' - sound familiar?). Buddha did not always sit under a tree - he walked and helped others. He found a beggar in his own body dirt, carried him to the river, washed and clothed him, and said, 'be kind always, because what you do to others comes to you'... Buddha's teachings are almost identical with Jesus' teachings.

*Jesus*
Archangel Gabriel recapped Jesus previous incarnations:

As Hermes, he knew how to manipulate energy. As Melchisedec, he took the spiritual to the ritual people would understand. As Joseph, he learned love and forgiveness. As Joshua, he went to the hidden places (Jericho) of consciousness and annihilated all error perception (negativity: 'tae no prisoners'). As Buddha, he learned how to discern what appears to be and what one needed to know what was real - the at-one-ment. Now he had to pull it all together... to establish forever the Christ Consciousness on Earth... It was not an easy task, and he needed helpers.

*Archangel Gabriel*
Jesus' mother, Mary, had been prepared to help him, even before he or she was born. When her time came, she did not realize it, so I came to her

and reminded her of what she had agreed to do, and said, 'Now!', and she rejoiced because she knew. (Mary's rejoicing is found in Luke 1:46-55). Jesus' molecular structure was in 2 states of consciousness at once. He had to focus on becoming a real person, and he had to focus on who he really is, and never lose his Christ Consciousness. He did 'practice runs' as a child - restoring to life a dead bird. When six years old, he was taken from the Essene community to India, where he was quite comfortable, since he had been there as Buddha. Then he went to Egypt.

Jesus traveled everywhere; he came to America. Jesus had free will, as we all do. When he went to the Jordan River to be baptized by John, they both knew the import of the pending event, and so John asked Jesus if he was sure, and Jesus said, Yes. (Scripture - *This is my son, in whom I am well pleased; hear ye him.* Matt 17:5)

The Christ energy was far beyond the realm of consciousness of Jesus, but went into the soul properties of Jesus… now there was a oneness that would never be gone. A divine connection was made; Jesus was transformed; all past [was] washed away. He needed to get used to it, so he went into the desert alone, [There is no Satan; the tempter was Jesus's ego self] and communed with angels and high masters until he could open this man in consciousness to the Christ, with nothing in between; to truly become the Son of God. He was shown all details of his future, to rejoice and weep, to walk through the fears of it, and come at last to inner peace.

When he came forth, he called forth the twelve disciples. They were all hand-picked, as were all the individuals in his life. Each apostle represents a faculty of man. These faculties are:

John - love
Matthew - will
Luke - light-giving
Simon Peter - faith
Andrew - strength
James, son of Zebedee ('James the less') - judgment
Philip - power
Bartholomew - imagination

Thomas - understanding
James son of Alpheus - order
Judas - life
Thaddeus - elimination

Gabriel described briefly some of the disciples: Peter was 100% behind Jesus as long as all went smoothly, but he had no conviction himself; thus denied Jesus three times. Thomas knew in theory what Jesus was doing, but had to see to believe. John was a sweet and gentle teenager, and had loved Jesus.

*Archangel Gabriel* (on Jesus meeting Mary Magdalene)... who was 'never a harlot'. She was wealthy with 'old money' and was asked by Jesus if she would 'make way for me and my students as we travel?' She agreed to, if he would take her as a student. He agreed.

At the crucifixion, Mary Magdalene was the last to leave the cross. In her desolation she hid away, then finally knew she had to go where he was. She was the first to see him risen, then Mother Mary, then Joanna (who told the disciples).

.... When he [Jesus] knew the crucifixion was coming, he knew what he needed to do, but he questioned his ability, and he knew he could not be in this doubting state of consciousness... angels were told to leave him alone. It was the hardest thing we [angels] ever did. He reviewed his life - John the Baptist, 'I am ready'. Under the water, where there was no earth sound; no breath, only God's Spirit. Out of the murky water; into the clarity of light and the warmth of day. Power came into him 'I am the begotten Son of God'. He called in that power, and again it manifested in him: 'the Father doeth the work'. Thus Jesus grounded forever this consciousness as your reality.

At the crucifixion, amidst all the grieving, Mother Mary was the only one who closed her eyes and thought 'This is the issue of Christ in form'. John took Mother Mary home, and then leaned on a wall and wept. Jesus came to him. John said, 'how can you be here when you are there?' Jesus said, 'I am the Son of God in truth. You behold an illusion. What you see [here] is I AM.' And John suddenly realized and understood.

He said, 'Then you live!'

And Jesus said, 'Indeed, I live.'

--------------------------------------------------------------------------

8/9/97 Pathways of the Mind
*Bible*
*For the thing which I greatly feared is come upon me, and that which I was*
*afraid of is come unto me.* Job 3:25

*Archangel Gabriel*
There is one mind; and there *aspects* of the mind: causal (generalities)
and concrete (specific thoughts). Other aspects are the rational and the
intuitive. [In] the rational mind: all conclusions are based on the past;
it is interested only in conclusions; [accepts] only the experiences of this
life (fear, jealousy etc). Thus it drags into your experiences all kinds of
blockages to prevent you from the joys of life, such as the inability to
move forward. It has he ability to go beyond limitations but chooses not
to. Your colleges, history, educational system cling to laborious blockages
of the past. From here comes the belief 'I can't do it'.

The intuitive mind does not reason; has no thinking rationale; is
completely enlightened; knows God, love, feelings; is the pure spirit Self
of you. It has no agenda; draws no conclusions; has no purpose to look to
the past for any guidance. It knows the only outcome must be good.

You created rational mind to get waylaid along the way. Intuition is
always there, always working. Remember: The spirit Self is reality; spirit
is the *real you*. In the days to come… you will need to use your intuition.
When you use the intuitive mind, you are living in the spirit.

*Author*
Many times Archangel Gabriel told us of the importance and power of
our thoughts. Negative thoughts bring negative experiences into our lives;
positive thoughts result in positive experiences. There is no such thing as
a neutral thought. Every thought is of a positive or negative nature. Our
thinking, rational mind often leads us down the negative road. We use

our rational mind constantly. We use it to remind self of the negative experiences of the past and base today's decisions on the past. It is circular thinking. What we fear comes to us, for the fear itself is an invitation to fear.

Focusing on anything will bring it to us, for thoughts are things. It is more productive, comfortable, and spiritual to ask for God's guidance. It is more sensible to use our intuitive mind, which is the Voice of God directing us. Faith is essential to rely totally on God's Guidance. When we consciously call on the Holy Spirit - the transforming energy of God - we are always guided on the path of truth; always. But the Holy Spirit only comes to those who seek Him.

-----------------------------------------------------------------------

*Bible*
*And the Word was made flesh, and dwelt among us, (and we beheld his glory, the glory as of the only begotten of the Father,) full of grace and truth.* John 1:14

*Archangel Gabriel:*
Your spirit self is curled up in a boat, asleep. I come now to awaken you to what you really are: children of God.

-----------------------------------------------------------------------

9/20/97 Transmutation of Energy
*And there arose a great storm of wind, and the waves beat into the ship, so that it was now full. And he was in the hinder part of the ship, asleep on a pillow; and they awake him, and say unto him, Master, carest thou not that we perish? And he arose, and rebuked the wind, and said unto the sea, Peace, be still. And the wind ceased, and there was a great calm.* Mark 4:37-39; Luke 8:23

*Archangel Gabriel*
When you awaken to the Son of God in you, that is the kind of command you will have. You will have control over all situations; all

emotions. You must bring in the transmutation of energy of the God Self of you... The true transformation of energy does not come from 'out there', but rather from within you. The greatest teacher that you will ever learn from dwells within you.

# CHAPTER TEN

# 1998

Reader please note: Although the focus of this book is Bible quotes and Gabriel's explanations, it also contains Jesus' own words as he came (1995-1999) to teach us about his life and his teachings. How blessed we were to be in his presence! Jesus presented this entire (all day) seminar, therefore only excerpts are offered.

*Opening remarks by Jesus the Christ:*
Peace be unto you, my brothers and sisters in the light. My heart is full of joy to see your faces, to be in your presence, to feel your love, to feel the bonding in fellowship one with another, in the Presence of God. I have long awaited this day in which I might come and gather with you here. My desire is not to speak of how I lived... much of what I taught on the Earth has been greatly misconstrued. It has troubled me all this time; that so much of the truth of it was left behind, and was made into what mankind thought should be said.

I have come in so many different forms, to so many people, in so many ways, to try to make right what was wrong. My desire this day is to straighten the crooked places; that the truth of what I brought might be fully understood and lived, and not be bound by the old ways.

*Author*
In this discourse, Jesus also spoke of mankind's journey to Earth, and our tendency to always look back. He noted how the Old Testament referred to 'James, the son of David',... 'the son of Abraham', etc., and always referred back; never forward. He mentioned the law of Vibration. He said our strong belief in bloodlines led to inter-marriage and sacrifice. He told of Moses' mission and the symbolism of the mountain. Moses believed in one God, but his perception of the truth of God came in rules and

regulations. 'Cast in stone' is unyielding; could not take in more; could not be changed. In speaking of Lots wife, Jesus said, "Whenever you rely upon the past to be your vehicle of truth, you are turned into salt. It is in the present moment that truth abides".

Jesus said that when he came he broke every rule; He loved openly; freely. He did not follow the rules of Moses, or the rules of the synagogue. "I didn't follow any rule except the internal rule of the Voice of my Father within me." He spoke of the inequality of the sexes: "Women were not equal with men, but they were to me... A man did not touch a woman in public; a man did not speak to a woman in public. Women were nothing more than possessions: someone to bear your children, cook your meal, and speak to you when asked to."

Jesus described the scene when he first met Mary Magdalene. He then spoke of the freedom we have yet to come to know: the freedom of love. "Not a freedom to go forth and hurt, but a freedom to go forth and love whoever you will, whether they love you back or not." He then said that within every human being there is a living spirit. It is the truth of us; it is the child of God of us. "That spirit in you is pure and holy; it knows no sin, it knows no error, it knows nothing of anything that would make you bad or wrong, or not what you should be. For that spirit is cast perfectly, absolutely perfectly, in the image and likeness of God."

Jesus described his apostles; their physical attributes their strengths and faults. He tells about his encounter [after his resurrection] with Saul. It is a fascinating tale of huge import, as it is the true story of the transformation of Saul into Paul. It, like all the teachings of Gabriel and Jesus, are recommended hearing/reading.

Jesus said, "Do you believe that God would send you anything that is not a blessing?" This phrase has become my [the author's] mantra, especially in times of obvious blessings and in those times when pain or limitation seem to be more a restriction than a blessing. Not long ago, as I was bemoaning to myself that I didn't much like using a walker to ambulate, the thought came to me, 'Where would you go - and why?' Now [using a walker], as I read these words of the Master, from January, 1998: "You don't have to walk fast to be on a spiritual path."

Archangel Gabriel and Jesus always took questions during their seminars. On this day, someone asked Jesus if he would clarify the misinterpretations in the Bible. He responded: "Only about three minutes would be needed to tell what was actually written, originally."

Then Jesus explained the real meaning of The Sermon on the Mount, (Matthew, Chapters 5-7). Jesus also spoke of losing his patience with his apostles. "They tried my patience greatly. And it was good that they did, because it kept me from becoming arrogant. You know, when you can do anything you want, and do it like that [snapping his finger] you have to be careful of arrogance; you really do. You have to be grounded in the spirit."

In response to a question about Pope Joan, Jesus said that she shaved her head (which a woman would never have done). She appeared rather masculine; commanding in appearance. They couldn't bear to have a female pope. She was a pope for only about two years. "That whole pope thing started with the idea that I said to Peter, 'You are a rock, and upon this I will build my church'.

"I never said any such thing. I did say to Peter, 'You are rather hard-headed, and upon this stubbornness you may build an edifice, which you will one day regret'. I loved Peter, but he was one of my biggest challenges... when he said to me, Thou art the Christ... he knew it with his head and not with his heart. And I said to Peter, 'You must learn to love'."

Jesus told about the woman who was about to be stoned for adultery [John 8:4-9]. "So I knelt down, and wrote the names of all the men there, and the dates when they were with this [or another] woman. And I invited them to look at what I had written. And they all came and looked. And I said, 'which one of you would like to cast the first stone?' And they couldn't, because they saw, in the writing on the ground, their own faces; their own guilt - and they walked away."

Jesus said that the disciples all agreed [to their roles] before coming to Earth. Jesus chose them because he knew that each had, in him, a wonderful gift to bring. When asked if he really wrote *A Course in*

*Miracles,* he said, "O, absolutely. She [Helen Shucman] was a tough customer... she didn't believe in me. That's what made her so good, because she never got into the emotional part of it... 'You're *who?*' And that was wonderful. Wonderful."

We often confuse truth with reality. Jesus clarified them for us: "The truth is, you are a child of God; you are spirit wearing a body. Reality is the ego taking the body here and there. Reality is what appears to be happening at the moment. Truth is *not* what is happening at the moment."

There are several pages of questions and answers. I give a few here. The reader is invited to hear/read the full tape/text. One of the questions was to summarize, in one sentence, his best advice to us now.

His answer: "Love God, love yourselves, love each other, and be joyful."

Q: If you had to do it all over again, what things would you have changed about your life on Earth?

A: The crucifixion. It was totally unnecessary.
This response may stun the reader, but in Gabriel' teachings he said Jesus' intent was indeed to save the world - *but only on the cross did he realize that he had only saved himself.* In truth, we each are our own savior.

Q: What was your biggest disappointment?
A: People.

Q: What was your greatest joy?
A: People.

Jesus described his women followers:
"'There were a lot of women who followed, but they were written out of your scriptures by a male-dominated world."

Jesus was asked about the method of death his disciples chose. He said, "Suffering serves no purpose in the sight of God. However, the human consciousness feels it must suffer to atone... You can choose to suffer or be joyful. You must practice to be joyful. It takes a concentrated effort, at first."

Another question was about the original Apostles Creed. It does not mention hell. Jesus responded, in part:
'To descend into hell is to descend into form, because form is limiting. This is the only hell there is; what you are in, right now. This is it.'

One of the many powerful statements of the Master was in response to a question about the Atonement:

"The true atonement is when you recognize that there is nothing to be forgiven for. Nor is there any ill that has been done to you. It's when you recognize that all of it was just an illusion and that, in truth, you never left home to begin with, and nobody has ever done anything to you or them that requires forgiveness. That is the ultimate forgiveness, when you realize there is nothing to forgive."

Regarding joy and the source of it, Jesus said,
"The Source of your joy comes from the God self of you; the spirit of you, from your own ability to recognize that you were created in such joy. We all were created in such joy, and to tap back into that joy is beyond anything. If one doesn't have joy within themselves, no partner in the world will bring them joy. Things don't bring you joy. Dedicated to possessions, you separate yourselves from your Source."

Closing prayer by Jesus the Christ:
*My Father, Oh Thou Whose voice speaks to the hearts of humankind; Your sweet whisperings,*
*Who pours the cooling waters of healing and truth into burning hearts of those who long to know.*
*Oh Thou, Whose strength created the Earth and caused the mountains to rise, Whose power molded the heavens, and brought into being life.*
*Oh Thou, Who are the Love that we express and know, the peace that we seek, and the joy that we are,*
*Oh Thou, most Wondrous, I give You thanks for this that has transpired this day.*

*I thank You for my brethren and sisters who have come to listen, to learn, to grow.*
*I thank You for this beloved instrument, who is an example of perfect trust in You, and in me.*
*I thank You for her loving arms that brought me comfort, and for her trust that teaches me Your love, even now.*
*I thank You that I AM, and that we are, in You, ever.*
*And so it is.*

# CHAPTER ELEVEN

# 1999

*Bible*
*And of his fullness have all we received, and grace for grace.* John 1:16

Although Gabriel did not quote scripture here, he did devote an entire all-day seminar to describing grace, explaining it, and telling us how to be aware of it. He defined grace as innocence; then defined innocence: "A state of being in which you are totally aware of your Christness; the Son of God of you, and you know that you have never done anything wrong."

The archangel assured us that grace is our natural state of being which we did not leave. There is no part of us that is not a part of God. "In this state of grace you are equal with all your brothers. You are unaware of earthly concerns. You are unaware of any illusions. You are unaware of anything below it." Gabriel told us that when Jesus healed he was in a state of grace. "The Holy Spirit operates from the state of grace, and in the emotional body you cannot reach the state of grace. But the Holy Spirit can reach it for you. The function of the Holy Spirit is to bring you back to God. Its method is love; its destination, atonement; its gift: perfect peace." In just one moment we can say, 'God, I want to come home to you'.

We have been taught for thousands of years that we are born in sin, Gabriel said. "Give up the treasures of your heart: pain, agony, suffering - all of which you bring to yourself." Gabriel reminded us of the Old Testament. 'What is wrong with your world? Read the Old Testament - in it God proclaims war (which God could never do), tells people to go to war, and all kinds of negative things. If you read the OT with *discernment*, it is a roadmap leading to the birth of Christ."

When humankind believed that God was external, we accepted the OT phrase 'no one ever looked upon the face of God and lived'. Now Gabriel tells us that every time we look at another we see God.

# THE
# REVELATION
# TO JOHN

# INTRODUCTION TO CHAPTERS 12-15

The interpretation of *Revelation* was transcribed directly from 6 audio-cassette tapes originally recorded, 3 tapes each day, on 1/25/92 and 2/22/92. At the request of Lucas, the *Good News Bible* was chosen. Lucas also requested that someone read from the Bible, and he would interpret paragraph by paragraph. Rev. Penny Donovan, beloved channel of Lucas, asked the author to read. I was thrilled at the honor. The words of the Bible are not found in this text. The reader is advised to read the *Revelation of John*. Lucas was/is Archangel Gabriel, but we learned that later, when he presented the lesson *Angels, Aliens and Earthlings* (7/27/91). Lucas prefaced his interpretation of *Revelation* with these words:

"Before we begin, let me tell you that *Revelation* is not about Mother Earth, nor is it the fatal collapse of human kind. It is not a time of sorrowing and suffering and great tribulation. It is a time of rejoicing; of coming forth and of being. It has always thought to be of the last days of the Earth, of damnation and hell-fire and all that sort of thing. The truth of it has never been understood. It has been taken in the context of the ego, and in the context of the ego it has been brought to a fear state of consciousness. And there is nothing further from the truth than that *Revelation* is of fear.

"Indeed, dearly beloveds, it is your story. It is the story of the man Jesus who came to the Earth to live an exemplary life, for you, in order that he, having lived in the flesh and having been subject to all the things of the flesh, might be able to give to you the pattern for you to follow. For one who has not been there, as it were, cannot give advice to another who is there, anymore than you can sympathize or empathize with someone in their tribulation if you have never known that tribulation. You can only sorrow from them and not from the standpoint of understanding.

"And so the Master Jesus took it upon himself to come unto the Earth in flesh in the most difficult time in history, and to ground thereon, the Earth Plane, the vibration of the Christ. He brought with him the living truth. And he knew that in order for him to make that living truth known, he had to live it, just as any ordinary man or woman would have to live it, and thusly he did. And it is from that concept of his journey that he was able to lay forth the path of your journey. And that is what *Revelation* is.

"Now we shall speak of all the things that are there, and that is why I had someone read it word for word. For you shall see, in its unfoldment, a reflecting glass, and you shall look into that reflecting glass and you shall behold it is your image and you shall see that *Revelation* has been written about you. I chose this day in your time to bring this truth unto you, for prior to this your heart and mind could not have comprehended that which I am about to bring to you. I had to wait for you to reach a point in your awareness for the words that I would teach you to take root and to grow. Otherwise they would have been like leaves in the wind, blowing thither and yon and lost to you forever, and requiring that in another lifetime you would have to learn what is the meaning of *Revelation*. And so it is, beloveds, that at this time your minds are ripe for the plucking. And in the days to come, of your time, you shall reap that which you sow from this day, in your understanding. We shall commence."

# Chapter Twelve - Rev., Chap. 1-5

<u>Revelation, Chapter One</u>

*Disciples.* a portion of consciousness. Each apostle represents a power of God. See Chapter Ten.

*Island of Patmo.* To return to the eternal Self, one must be separated entirely from anything of the Earth. A singleness of purpose. A State of consciousness, in which nothing of the Earth pulled at him.

*Angels.* creative ability

Archangel Gabriel is the angel of the Annunciation; messenger; to teach and open hearts and minds.

*Head angels (archangels) E*ach pours fourth 7 other angels, then each of 7 pours forth 7 more etc. etc., to thousands of angels. The seven archangels were described by Gabriel on July 27, 1991. Their names and functions follow, but the reader is encouraged to read/hear the seminar for more details:

Archangel Gabriel: Angel of Annunciation. To teach humans
Archangel Michael: Warrior angel [not human warfare]
Archangel Raphael: Healer
Archangel Uriel: Angel of repentance
Archangel Zadkiel: Angel of Joyous Mercy and Benevolence
Archangel Metatron: Angel of Spiritual Sustenance
Archangel Ariel: Angel of Emotions

Also, Gabriel said there are seven Dominions of angels:
Seraphim: Angels of the First Cause
Cherubim: Perfect record Keepers
Thrones: Keepers of the Flame of Life
Dominions: Assignors of Angelic Duties
Virtues: Angels of Miracles

*Rev. Ellen Wallace Douglas*

Powers: Angels of Planetary Changes
Principalities: Angels of Spiritual Pathways

*Seven churches.* states of consciousness (we all have them).
We must pass through each state of consciousness, by fasting (from negation on any level) and constant prayer.

*King.* state of mind; an attitude form.

*coming in clouds.* Your blurred vision of who you are.

*coming through clouds.* awareness of the Christ in you.

*Alpha and omega.* The number ten is a circular number. Its two parts are:

1 - (pillar) masculine; action, that which moves upon

0 - (circle) feminine; that which is moved upon, nurturing

*snow-white hair.* highest attainment; purist pure; 7th chakra, at crown of head

*eyes that burn.* clear vision; fullness of knowing

*face shone like the sun.* face (presented to the world); the sun (light of the world; Christ)

*feet like burned brass.* feet = understanding; polished understanding, so he knew all things made from the spirit of livingness. All the experiences Jesus had brought him to the Christ Light.

*Two-edged sword.* The voice of truth.

Your words are very powerful. The power of the spoken word is a declaration, and so it shall be unto you. 'I AM ---' can proclaim positive or negative. Daily you use both, without thinking.

*I was dead.* You are *all* dead in Christ; have not come into the fullness of knowing who you are. You are sacred. Scripture: *Because I live, you shall live.* Jesus lived through all life's experiences and came out of it, just as you shall.

*They are liars.* The Christ within cannot bear that which is not perfect. Love and hate cannot co-exist. Jesus took many lifetimes to reach the point of becoming Christ. In his last lifetime he embraced all errors of the past, through actions of others to him. All wounds are self-inflicted. Jesus "suffered" to show you how unnecessary it is.

Revelation, Chapter Two - Seven Churches

1.  Ephesus - Desirable; appealing

*What I have against you; you do not love me as you did at first*

When you first come into your truth, do you not want it more than anything else in the world; willing to sacrifice anything for it; you want to tell everyone? That lasts about a fortnight, then it begins to dwindle, and the zeal has begun to fade. Know you how far you have fallen? Until you get up there, you can't fall, can you? You are tip-toeing into your Christness, and from that point you fall down and down; some further than others.

*I will give you the right to eat the fruit of the tree of life.* Coming forth into your knowingness. How can you eat the fruit of something that you do not know exists? Overcoming your lack of enthusiasm and regaining it. You taste life (with enthusiasm). Do you know anyone who is unenthusiastic and tastes of life? The person who has a zeal for life knows the fruits of the tree of life.

2.  Smyrna. The intellect; your mind; that part of you which knows.

The 'downside' of that is your reasoning mind. You reason away truth, argue for your limitations - and you get to keep them. In your spiritual selves you have the Mind of God. In that mind you know all things. Your ego would have you believe you are stupid; that you do not know all things; you are easily victimized by others because you don't know what they are doing. It also would have you believe in limitation. You are limited: 'I cannot learn this; I can't do that because I don't know how'. 'I cannot change my life because I don't know how', etc.

'I don't know how' is probably one of the most frequently used phrases in your world. That is the ego-self of you speaking, for the God-mind of you knows how to do anything.

*will last ten days.* Here comes the number ten again.

*I know that you are poor.* How many here think you are poor in spirit? Everybody! If you didn't think that, you wouldn't be here, and I wouldn't be standing here teaching you. In truth, you are rich, for you have all gifts of The Father, have you not?

*those who claim to be Jews but are not.* Jews are *symbolic* of the chosen of God. They are those who would attend your churches every Sunday, and then go home and beat their wives. Those who would teach little children in Sunday school, and then take a little girl out behind a building and rape her. Those who proclaim the Christ is alive and well, and then go out and beleaguer their neighbor; say evil things. They are the egos of all of you that would teach you anything that is not of God. They are the ones who claim to be that which they are not.

*the devil.* That self of you which would convince you that you are not worthy.

*thrown into prison.* prison = limitation

*ten days.* alpha and omega: Source from which all things proceed and the end to which all things return. You will stay in the prison until you have made the circle and return to your Source. Are you beginning to get it?

*Be faithful to me even if it means death.* Here is where the people of the Earth got the idea that it was wondrous indeed to be a martyr. The birth of martyrdom! The death means the death of everything you cherish in your error perceptions; your perception of what you *think* life is. It is easier to be a victim than to break [through your knowingness] the chains that bind you. The death that is threatened here is the death of the ego. It is the second death, for it is the memory of your soul, which is imperfect. And believe me, it is not painful. The soul of you is the memory of you. The memory from the moment the Father brought you forth, the remembrance of the ego which would have you not know who you are. The ego throws up a smoke screen and takes from your sight the truth of you. The ego has you believe that you must come and pay a debt lifetime after lifetime after lifetime, for ever and ever. The soul of you records all that is in your feeling nature. If you carried not in the heart of your being your treasure (which is your memory), you would be at one with the Father!

3.  Pergamum. The emotional state of you. Your feeling nature is your intuition; the God Self of you. The downside of that is your emotions. When you are in an emotional state of upset, you cannot see truth, for it is a blinding light. It sees only what it desires to express.

*Antipas.* [was a disciple]. [He] defended a myth because he believed Jesus to be the *only* son of God. He believed with the totality of his being that Jesus was the Christ. But he never saw the truth of what Jesus taught. Antipas suffered pain, through annihilation, until he was martyred. He represents a state of mind best described as blind faith.

*Nicolaitins.* Mixed thought. You cannot make up your mind. You believe you can make a mistake. This causes you to make error upon error. You do not trust the God of you enough to decide something and stay with it.

*food that had been offered to the idols.* All of you worship idols. Your biggest idol is fear. You fear you will not be healthy, you will not make enough money, the decisions you make will be wrong. You fear what your neighbor is going to do with something he possesses; you fear you cannot keep that which you treasure. You fear you will displease another; you will lose someone you love; your little creatures will not be well in your absence, etc. etc.

*manna from Heaven.* Learning how to live from the Lord God of your Being. Knowing that you are totally self-sufficient within you and you do not need what the world offers.

*the white stone upon which is written a name.* The white stone is the symbol of your internal self. The tablets upon which the Ten Commandments were written. You are the Son of God and that is the name written upon the stone. Each of you is called by a sound; it is your own sound; the ring of truth. The Lord God of your Being calls unto you.

4. Thyatira. Represents your understanding; the church of desire. 'Desire' means de (from) sire (the Father).

*Jezebel.* That aspect of your desire that would lead you astray; tells you that instant gratification is okay, regardless of the results. Ex: food, purchasing unnecessary things.

*I will throw her on a bed.* The bed of regret. Immorality is adulterating a gift of God. You have brought it down into the abyss.

*the deep secrets of satan.* 'Why not [do it]? Nobody is going to know' attitude. The Jezebel state of mind.

*authority over the nations.* The nations' represent every aspect of your being: spiritual, emotional, feeling nature, mind - everything! 'authority over them' - every aspect that you are using at that moment, is under the Christ influence and not under ego.

*break them like clay pots.* Illusions; nothingness. Thoughts are things. Most of what you honor in life as being important has little value. Until you come into that state of awareness where you recognize this, you will honor clay pots.

*give them the morning star.* The morning star is the first glimmering of awareness that you are more than what you thought you were, that you are not your body, your thoughts, your emotions. You are nothing less than the Son of God. The morning star gives forth a brighter light than the night stars, but it is dimmed by the sun. The rising sun [means] the coming into the fullness of your Christhood.

Revelation, Chapter 3

5.  Sardis. A combination of things within you: intellect, knowing, understanding, feeling nature (intuition), desire to continue on your path. All these things in your life seem to fluctuate.

*wake up!* Reconnect with that center of you; your Source!

*Remember where you came from.* You came from the Father.

*come upon you like a thief.* Would take from you your grandest treasure: your fear.

*thief in the night.* Night - dark aspect of the soul. Thief- that state of mind in which Christ would come and take away what you hold dear - all your limitations, *which do not exist except in your mind.* The Christ will take away your limitations and give you Light.

*clothed like this in white.* Come into your fullness of the Spirit of God within you.

*remove their names from the book of the living.* If a person is not aware of life, they are said 'to not be written in the book of life'. How could someone not be aware of life? Those who perceive selves in abject poverty; poverty of the internal self. Those who do not use their creative imagination; who stumble from one day to the next; eyes cast down; their awareness darkened.

6.  Philadelphia. Love. It is not by accident that you have a city by that name.

*The key that belonged to David.* David is a lesser aspect of the Christ. David was a warrior, but he loved God greatly. His warrior state of mind led him to un-God like things. [You need] the tenacity to hold fast to the love of God.

*keep you safe from the time of trouble.* What aspect of your beingness gets you into the most trouble? Is it not love turned upon itself in error?

Addiction - the greatest one is addiction to fear. You love to be scared to death - TV; movies; roller coasters. You love the fear that gives you a thrill, and thus you feed the idol of fear.

*I know that you have a little power.* Love is the most powerful force in the world; you all have love. Yet you perceive yourselves to be powerless.

*I have opened a door before you which no one can close.* The door of love! No one can shut it, but you. No one makes you stop loving them, except you. It is you who decide not to love them. Love never stops; it is forever and ever. You may lose interest, but the love goes on always.

*test all the people on Earth.* Every day you test yourselves; you beat upon yourselves.

*I shall make them bow down before you.* All your perceived error thoughts that have caused you to think ill of yourselves will have to be reckoned with by the Christ, and they cannot stand before Him.

*I will write on him the name of my God.* The name of God is Love!

*the New Jerusalem*

[The] internal Self of you, having been redeemed of all its error perceptions - and brought into the Light in its totality.

7.  Laodicea. That aspect of your being which is Knowingness. The downside is belief. When you *believe*, you are manifesting that which has no solidness behind it. When you *know* something, you are basing it on spiritual truth.

*We think you are rich when in truth you are poor.* Material things are ever changing; never the same; transitory. Belief in material life is to deny your spirituality.

*I shall spit you out of my mouth.* Mouth: you put in beliefs and digest them; they become part of you, and from you come your proclamations.

'I am (this) or (that)'. To cast from your knowingness all error perceptions that would have you think [that] a non-truth is a truth.

*Beasts*. The beasts of the earth are those things of the earth which you think are real: jobs, homes, marriages, relationships; all [are] based upon earthly things. The birds are the powers that are there for you to use, that you have not yet formed into anything.

Revelation, Chapter 4

*I saw an open door in Heaven*. The door to [a State of] Heaven is bringing yourself up into the Highest of consciousness. You do not think of the spiritual or of eternal things.

*there in Heaven was a throne*. The throne is the 7$^{th}$ (crown) chakra; at the top of the head. The seat of intuition. The absolute sureness within you.

*twenty-four elders seated around*. The twelve aspects (virtues) of humans - John is love, Peter is faith, etc (see Chapter Ten) have two sides (24). The perfect balance of love are the male (action) and the female (sustaining). All these virtues must come into balance.

*Thunders and lightnings*. What I [Gabriel] know to be harmony. Your ego self perceives thunder and lightning; your ego self cannot hear the harmony.

*sea of glass*. The sea of Earth is a moving thing; all rhythms of your life - action and repose. The sea of glass is the perfect balancing; the stillness.

*looked like a lion*. Lion [represents] fearlessness. The lion has very few natural enemies, save man. To become fearless you have to have absolute trust in the Father.

*looked like a calf*. It should read 'bull'. Bull is strength; the strength in God.

*like a man's face*. Face- what you present to the world. No one has a face like yours. Behind it is the Is-ness of you. It is your uniqueness.

*fly like an eagle.* [The] eagle flies higher than any other bird; has a keen eyesight. You are limitless and boundless. Flight - you are not bounded; nothing limits you. You are free in Christ.

*had eyes before and aft.* The all-knowingness of your beingness. Eyes- [the] Self; all-knowing; able to perceive and see; to take into.

*holy, holy, holy, is the Lord God Almighty.* This is you! holy, holy, holy is the Lord God of your Being. It is your divine nature. You are the Son of God; and that is honoring that.

*they threw their crowns before the throne.* Crowns [are] accomplishments.

*casting down before the throne.* 'All I have gained is of God'. When you have accomplished the fullness of each of those aspects (virtues), your are given a crown of accomplishment. To offer it before the throne is to know that whatever you give to God is returned to you a thousand fold.

Revelation, Chapter 5

*the seven seals.* the seven aspects of you; the chakras. Seven is the number of completeness.

*There was no one in Heaven or Earth who could open the seals.* No one else has your memory; no one. Only you can open the seals; with the fearlessness of a lion, and fear not what it will behold. What you have made is karma. You created karma; not God. You took the law of Cause and Effect and adulterated it. [You made of] it a reward and punishment; God did not. Breaking the seals means freeing yourselves from the wheel of karma, forever.

*The lamb appeared to have been killed.* The willingness of Jesus, who embodied the Christ, to come to Earth. And your willingness to be killed to the lesser; the lower; that which is limitation.

*priests.* The individual who has dominion over the lesser

*from every tribe, language, nation, and race.* Every state of consciousness. Your awareness of what you perceive to be sin. "[your] awareness of worry, anxiety, warfare, lack, hatred, anger, jealousy. On the spiritual plane, your denial of God by clinging to the soul, which is the memory of all things, including error, which is *not real.*

<u>verses 11-14.</u> This is the completion of your awareness. 'I am God! I am the Son of God.!' It is your recognition of that divinity. You know it, but have not brought it into action.

# Chapter Thirteen: Rev., Chap. 6-14, v.5

Now the story of you using this, and the journey that it takes you through - the valley of shadows; the abyss.

<u>Revelation, Chapter Six</u>

*I saw the lamb break open the first of the seven seals.* I'll speak of one seal at a time. Seals represent what you do not want to look at - not because it hides a terrible thing, but [because] it hides your own glory. Your greatest fear is that you are indeed the son of God.

*Seal 1. A white horse. Its rider held a bow, and he was given a crown.* White is the color of purification. The rider has brought every experience and purified it; brought it up into the light.

*he went out as a conqueror.* He is a conqueror. This is the story of you.

*Seal 2. Another horse came out; a red one.* Red is the color of anger; color of emotion. You have a saying, 'I saw red'. Red is also the color of energy. In its pureness it is bright and good. The emotional body with all its rages, makes war on the Self of you. The Christ of you is ever defending itself against the ravages of the beast in you - that ego which makes war upon the Christ.

*Seal 3. The lamb broke the third seal. There was a black horse.* Black does not denote evil, but protection. This is the reasoning mind. You have the concept that you must 'earn your living'. God gives you livingness. The Law of Limitation and the law of Karma, both of which you created, deny your natural right and you believe you must pay for things. You should live in abundance from the Lord God of your Being, not deprived, as a bag lady, a 'bum', etc. You have created a black place where you have hidden away all your good.

*Seal 4. The lamb broke open the fourth sea... a pale colored horse. Its rider was named death. And hades followed close behind.* The horse and rider represent your belief in limitations (illness, war, plague etc). Only in the ego is there death. When you listen to the ego you believe the illusions that you are faced with. When [you are] in tune with the Father, and know your own Christhood, you are not subject to the illusions.

*Seal 5. The fifth seal.* The aspect of you that seeks revenge.

*was given a white robe… rest a little awhile longer.* The Christ within you needs time to be rested and allowed to nurture and bring forth, and eliminate the idea in your consciousness, of revenge.

*the voice crying out.* The Voice of The Christ, eager to come forth and manifest.

*Seal 6. stars falling from Heaven.* Divine ideas coming down into your mental receptivity.

*sun became black.* You are not allowing the Christ in you to shine forth into your awareness.

*moon turning red.* The moon is the planet of emotion. Ever noticed how everybody is a little loony at a full moon? The moon's pull makes the tides. Nothing is more powerful than the pull of emotion.

*the sky… like a scroll being rolled up.* Sky - powers you have, to draw upon. You have turned your thoughts away from your Source, and are not aware of it. It does not exist for you; it is rolled up; not there.

Revelation, Chapter Seven

*no wind would blow on the earth, sea, or tree.* Winds represent change. When you think you 'know it all' you do not allow winds of change to bring you anything further.

*coming from the east.* East is the direction of illumination: the sun rises; truth comes forth. The illuminating aspect of your mind.

*power to destroy.* Your creative mind has the power to do *anything.* You have set it upon a deep path of destruction, illness, limits.

*power to damage the earth.* Do not harm the Earth. Earth represents the nurturing aspect of your nature; the mother aspect - the giving birth, the bringing forth, the sustaining.

*Mark of the Lord upon their heads.* The third eye [sixth chakra]. Limitless vision to understand all things.

*It was 144,000.* 144,000 comes to the number nine, [which is] the number of mankind's evolution. The spiral goes upward. From here on, in Revelation, every figure adds to nine.

*people too numerous to count.* All the creative ideas you have manifested, gathered together, redeemed through growth, progress, the evolution upward, and brought before the throne of God.

*who are these people?* The ego says 'I don't know' because the ego cannot recognize the totality of God; but any one of the elders would.

*the people who have come safely through the great persecution.* Ask yourself: How many tribulations have you already come through? You have remained faithful through them all and have come before the throne. You are well on your way; otherwise you wouldn't be here.

Revelation, Chapter Eight

*Seal 7. silence in heaven for about half an hour.* How many minutes in an hour? Sixty; half is thirty. Thirty makes three, the number of the Trinity: Father, Son, Holy Spirit - or body, mind and spirit. The silence in the three is the abidingness of God, Who never abandons you. The silence is not non-movement. It is a stillness that your minds could not comprehend at this time. It is the living Presence of God.

*had a gold incense container.* Incense is the source (creative thought) that wafts its way up into a higher place in [your] consciousness. You may call it prayer.

*fire from the altar.* the fire of life; the burning desire *to be.* It is the all-consuming flame of Christ that burns away anything not pure and holy.

The desire of life itself to be. Life is God in action.

*thunder, lightning, an earthquake.* Dissolving limitations; breaking away anything that is not flowing with the life of God. Breaking up all the error perceptions; the wretched thought forms you have built and turned loose on Earth.

*a third of the earth was burned up.* Three Again - the Trinity. Not destruction against mankind. It is the opposite. It is the Elohim. It is the spirit that pours itself forth limitlessly upon the Earth. It is life.

*mixed with blood.* Not [referring to] slaughter. New blood is brought into a situation to improve it. Breeders of little creatures use new blood to improve.

*then the second angel blew his trumpet. A large mountain was thrown into the sea.* The sea represents the psychic aspect; the astral plane. Some psychics use 'showmanship', to selfishly seek praise. The sea is ever moving; it is the source of life on Earth, from a physical standpoint. The Lord Christ said, 'If you have faith you shall say unto the mountain cast ye into the sea and it will obey'. When you take away the mountain of limitations in your path, you will re-awaken to the Trinity *in you.*

*a large star dropped from the sky... a third of the water turned bitter.* Stars - divine ideas - brought down to earth, and used for malice, are bitter. Love can turn bitter when one stops caring about another.

*star of bitterness.* Unforgiving people are beneath it.

*rivers and springs.* Rivers and springs of life energy - with negativity, are also made bitter.

*their light lost a third of its brightness.* When you do not tune into that center of Light within you, which is God, you are denying the very flow of your Essence to you. There has to be that connection between the

Father (Source of all), the Son (which is you), and the Holy Spirit (the action of the divine); otherwise your Light cannot shine.

*an eagle flying high in the air.* perception in is clarity. Stepping away from a situation (rising above it) helps one to see more clearly. The clear vision of intuition. Recognizing that all your horrors are of your own creation.

## Revelation, Chapter Nine

*key to the abyss.* An abyss is a bottomless pit. Nothing is better symbolized by 'abyss' than the memory of you souls, for your memories go back forever; they are indeed a bottomless pit.

*fifth angel blew his trumpet and the abyss was opened.* The Voice of God calling you back; calling you Home. Let go forever of your soul's memory and return unto the Father.

*smoke upon the earth.* If you allow fear to govern you, (you do not let go of soul's memory) the smoke will cloud your vision.

*pain one suffers when stung by a scorpion.* What stings more than regret? Your conscience will devour you, like locusts; with the sting of a scorpion. People have committed suicide through nothing more than the pain of regret.

*number 5.* The number five used to be considered the number of evil. It is the number of balance between one and ten. The number five is also the number of transformation.

*the locusts looked like horses.* Horses signify emotions; the feeling nature.

*hair like a woman.* growth and intuition. 'Hair is a woman's crowning glory', it was once said. There was an ancient law about women not cutting their hair, since it meant to cut off her intuition. Samson, believing his strength was in his hair, believed himself to be weak without it.

*chariots racing through the air.* This does not refer to airplanes that drop bombs. It is the flight of thought which, in its power, is able to destroy.

*release the four angels who are bound.* Release of creative thought; set free again.

*and the sulfur coming out.* The nose is connected to your ability to taste. You should taste life, not garbage.

*Smoke.* Obliterates sight

*a third of the human race was killed.* Takes away - kills - error perception, that robs you of your ability to create consistently. Your memory of error holds you to the wheel of karma; keeps you going past it with your emotions (horses).

*why did you not stop worship of the demons?* You are slow learners. You return again and again, a little higher than before. You no longer burn people at the stake, but you drop a bomb on them. You no longer have slavery, but you pay women less, etc.

Revelation, Chapter Ten

*angel and little scroll.* Your creative ability is limitless. When you connect your many inconsistencies to intuition (the sea), you can manifest anything you desire.

*Scroll.* It represents that creative ability which you have.

*take and eat the scroll.* Ingesting means it nourishes you. When ideas are God-based they do not turn sour. You have done some terrible deeds in the name of God.

*holy city for 42 months.* (42x30=1260 = 9). Nine again.

Revelation, Chapter Eleven

*two witnesses.* Wisdom and love.

*Fire.* The consuming love of Christ which embraces all things and drives out all negation through its transformation.

*to shut up the sky; no rain.* Means to not allow anything to wash from man's consciousness the truth of his being. Rain can be a blessing or curse. It nourishes earth, and it also floods.

verses 7-14. Pretty grisly, eh? More numbers: seven is a sacred number. Ten is completion. Three- and- a- half is half of seven; half of the truth. Wisdom and love are often seemingly killed. Have you not seen it? The ego rejoices in it. When you use wisdom you are using the Lord God of your Being. Another seems to 'wound' you and you say it's okay, but inside a resentment is brewing. You only have half the truth.

*Covenant Box.* The Covenant of God. The promise of God that is Life.

*rainbow about his head.* The rainbow is symbolic of the Covenant of God. The innermost color of the rainbow is green (color of healing, harmony, peace) and all other colors proceed from it.

*violent earthquake.* An earthquake is the shattering of old beliefs. In the area of an earthquake, there is wherein the thought forms need to be broken away.

Revelation, Chapter Twelve

*woman clothed like the sun.* The woman is the Mary aspect of you; pure center of innocence; of absolute love, capable of conceiving and bringing forth the Christ.

*dragon.* The dragon represents the ego. It waits for a new idea about the Christ, and kills it. Your great ideas are shattered by the negativity of the ego.

*the woman gave birth to a son.* The Son of God.

*the desert.* Nothing being produced (created).

*Woman.* Sustaining abilities; state of spirituality; ego did not pursue it, because it saw no value in pursuit.

*war broke out in Heaven.* This is your Armageddon that you are told of. Here is a situation where Heaven is, being the state of evolvement, state of mind, of consciousness, of Beingness - in which all things are of a spiritual nature, when you are at-one-ment with the Father - and the ego [dragon] will try to pull you out of it.

But *Michael* says 'Who is like unto God?' Your Michael aspect recognizes your own divinity, and the surliness; emptiness of the ego.

*the accuser of our brothers.* The accuser is your ego self.

*blood of the lamb.* Lambs are little, defenseless creatures; depend totally on shepherds. You take in 'new blood' and uplift the human race with Christ consciousness.

*lamb of God.* Pure innocence that is totally dependent upon the Father. In its pureness it is safe in the Father's care.

*those who be glad they died.* Death of ego ideas.

*the devil.* There is no physical devil; there is no spiritual devil, either.

*pursuit of the woman.* The ego always pursues that which will nurture the Christ, because it knows with the life of the Christ, the ego is dead.

*seashore* - psychic field; astral field.

The dragon sent water to wash away, with a softness (represent mediums who use ability to pull down mankind by selfish gains). Those who practice black magic, burn black candles, etc. are unevolved.

Revelation, Chapter Thirteen

*a beast.* The beast is fear. Greed is a form of fear.

*came up out of the earth.* Purely materialistic. Dictators. (Hitler).

*all the little people.* It takes all the little people to form the masses and it takes the masses to form the attitude form.

*people living on the earth.* Those in a state of realization (not consciously) that they are more than a body; more than what they appear to be.

*being written in a book.* An ancient memory - unconsciously - of their [higher] Selves.

*meant to be captured.* Allow selves to be entrapped by ide as of limitations (illness, failure, death, poverty, etc.

Revelation, Chapter Fourteen

*Its number is 666.* Nine again; evolution of mankind. Mass consciousness of need. You allow your corporate minds to influence the way you live. Some aspect of you knows you are wealthy. The imbalances in your world is the beast that you flee from. Helping poor countries is not the answer. The God of you seeks ever to give to that poor aspect of you, and bring you up into the embrace of the Father. Bring that 'poor child' of you home to the abundance, and then you will find no more hunger anywhere on Earth.

*sexual relations with women.* Does not refer to literal sexual encounters. Joining with another in a sexual act is more than physical. It is an exchanging of energies. Once joined in copulation, you are joined with that person, on that energy level, for a very, very, very long time. It is one of the most binding things you can do. You are unifying; joining on a psychic level. Its source is the same as the source of the kundalini, and the kundalini is as close as you are going to get to pure divine energy incarcerated in physical form. The problem with that is, joining with various and sundry others, you deplete yourself. When you [have sex] with the same person over and over you have the tree of life on the ethers; many partners simply depletes energy. That is why the Bible condemns harlots; whores. That is why the Bible says a man should not waste his seed, for he is wasting the energy of life.

-------------------------------------------------------------------------

Following are excerpts from the question and answer period after Gabriel's lecture on Part One of Revelation:

Q. Why are we so afraid to know we are children of God?

A. Because you would have to give up your soul, your memories and you believe that your past is you, and if you give up the past you will no longer be. You fear the power that goes with it (knowing you are the son of God). So you play the victim role over and over again, to prove you are powerless. You believe you are married to your past and you are not. When you see the nothingness of it (your past) and begin in the pure innocence of your being the Son of God; you begin again. This is what is meant by being 'born again'. Live from the Lord God of You. That's all it takes. The idea of death stems from the ego, which created Karma. The power of the Living God lives within you, and the result of that power is love. A holy, blessed love, that neither wounds nor is wounded, that neither causes grief nor is grieved. That brings forth blessings multi-fold; that heals, sustains, and lives in you, as you allow it to be so.

Every religion that has been created by man, has been created in a state of separateness. And then came one [Jesus] who came back to show the unification of all humankind, and he did it without mystery. But it was in the simplicity of the love of God which he came. 'What I have done, you can do also,' said he. As long as you walk through the abyss, angels of light will come and show you the way. But we cannot make you walk in the way. We can only show you the way. We present to you the gate, but you must walk through it. We can offer to you the stairway, but you must climb it. We can give you life in its understanding, but you must live it.

# CHAPTER FOURTEEN - REV. CHAP. 14, v.6 - 17

<u>Revelation, Chapter 14 continued</u>

*Heaven, earth, sea and water.* These refer to the spiritual, mental, emotional and physical aspects of humans. 'Fear God' is a misconception of your words. It should be 'Love God'. To love God means to love every aspect of your own being. You are God out-pictured. Recognize your own divinity, as Son of God. There is nothing separate from God.

*Babylon.* A state of consciousness which is confusion (tower of Babel). Confusion of earthly and spiritual thoughts; most religions dwell there.

*Babylon has fallen.* When confusion, misunderstanding, error perceptions all come to an end, and there is a clarity of understanding.

*fire and smoke.* Fire. the consuming passion to own, control, have power. Smoke blurs vision. Burning within the human soul to have, have, have earthly things (illusions). Greed is rampant upon your Earth. Corporate minds and little people: money equals power, and there are those who can reach across the world and change the life of others. They rule the 'little people' who have power, but do not know it.

*'faithful to Jesus'* should be *'faithful to the Christ'.* Hold fast to that which you know to be the Christ, the spirit within you. You do not have to be a Christian to practice Christ awareness.

*die in service to the Lord.* This is mistakenly understood to mean that martyrdom is glorious. It is a total waste. Die to the memory of your soul, which is the memory of all your past: your perceptions, false or true. To be unaware of error perceptions, but remember the experiences for what they have taught you. It is untrue that you were born sinners. Ego believes in limitation; spirit [knows] no limits. Fear is ego's favorite weapon.

*Sickle.* Your ability to separate truth from error.

*City.* [The] spiritual aspect of you in your purity; that which came directly from Divine Essence.

*outside of the city.* Where you have ventured forth [to Earth], to your little experiences. Where you are gleaning and learning; growing and becoming. You bring that all back and this is how you become God, in your knowingness.

*New Jerusalem.* The totality of your being. Every aspect of you, including the energy cells of our body.

*pressing out and it became blood.* [To] strengthen, as when a species is genetically altered; to press that out.

*floods out a great distance and is deep.* [The] flow of the essence of life, and you have to rid it of the impurities.

Revelation, Chapter Fifteen

*God's wrath.* God has no wrath. It means the spiritual aspect of you recognizes the inconsistencies of the ego's teachings.

*sea of glass.* Clarity of perception.

*Fire.* Zeal for life; the consuming flame of Christ. Burns away the dross, and allows that which is to be purified, and brought into an even better clarity.

*song of Moses; song of the Lamb.* Moses represents law; Law of Cause and Effect. Effect which you have brought down into the baser idea of karma. Law of the Lamb - Law of Love. Higher, spiritual laws.

*King.* State of consciousness. There are many states of consciousness; you are aware of so few of them. They could go on forever; you have no words to explain it.

*all the nations.* Every aspect of your being. The states of awareness of you: physical, mental, emotional, etheric, spiritual, forms of your space, time, timelessness, spacelessness, that which you used to be, are now and perceive self to become in the future.

*temple in Heaven; temple of God.* The sanctuary of your knowingness, in which you are one with the Father.

*Covenants of God.* Out-pictured on your earth plane.

*Tabernacle of God.* Contains the tablets upon which were supposedly written the Ten Commandments. The knowingness which knows that the things of limitation, of the ideas and the ideals of the ego have to be banished; have to be gotten rid of. And the only way they can be gotten rid of is to be faced head-on. The angel came forth from the tabernacle of God. It was the angel of your creative ability to survive.

*clean shining linen.* Purity of the knowingness of that moment; it is untouched by anything that is not joy.

*seven centers of consciousness.* The chakras - in the etheric form - influence the physical form at the endocrine glands.

Revelation, Chapter 16

*Seven plagues; bowls of God's wrath.* The first plague is lust. Not just sexual; anything of a physical nature. Lust is desire turned upon itself in negativity. Desire is a very pure and holy thing; that which causes you to become more. But when you take that pure spiritual aspect of you and bring it down into pure lust you have adulterate it. You have despoiled the sanctuary."

The second plague is greed. The difference between lust and greed: Lust wants something but doesn't always want to keep it. Greed holds onto and wants to keep it. Greed will dry up anything. Life is a flowing, and to hoard is to stop the flow.

The third plague is fear. It is the ego's only weapon.

*poured out the blood of God's people.* Since your first day s on Earth, when you hunted dinosaurs, we presented truth to you. Entities have come to Earth in physical from to bring you truth, and with few exceptions all of them have been slaughtered. Behind that is the killing by the ego of the spirit of truth. The ego will ever seek to murder that which will make it lesser. Blood is the life force of the physical form and the symbology of it is the spring of life - the spirit within you.

The fourth plague is remorse.

*poured out his bowl on the sun.* The sun represents the intellect. [It is] your ability to learn and understand.

*burned by the fierce heat.* Is anything more burning than the feeling of remorse? 'If only I had said; done; otherwise'.

The fifth plague is materialism.

*bit their tongues.* Tongue - ability to express. What has been expressed upon your earth? All of the undesirable things. The only thing that matters is what you can get while on earth. This is poured out on Earth by corporations which say 'buy, buy, buy'. I am against corporations as they are. The concept was good, but it went awry.

*the beast.* Is a conglomeration of a coming together of all the seven plagues of lust, greed, fear, etc.

The Sixth plague is limitation.

*River Euphrates.* Represents the law of supply: physical, as food; mental, as in fluxing of ideas, inspirations; emotional, as ability to love, accept love, to praise and be praised, to give and to receive. Your connection with the spiritual is drying up. it has dried up. Reason for this: rampant on Earth is idea of limitation. When you perceive your world is coming to a grinding halt, that is what you are going to get. It has already begun.

Because you have lost the ideal of constant supply, and have locked into the idea of limited supply. The ozone layer is getting bigger. Your state and those around it are prime targets for the ozone hole.

Great corporations will come crashing down. This is necessary because only in the breaking away from the *separation*, can the birthing of *unification* come to be. There has to come a unification upon your Earth; the unification of *all* people. This means recognition of the differences as a complimentary, an infusion into the whole of humankind. Race consciousness has to be changed. It has to grow into the ability to see, and say 'yes, my neighbor is different, but bless that difference'.

In scripture it says 'make way for the kings from the East.' The East is illumination; enlightenment. The old way of thinking is drying up. In its place is coming 'the kings from the East', or your ability to tune into the law of supply. This will turn you world around. Live in your knowingness and you shall see only with your eyes the fruits of the labors of those who do not practice spirituality.

*Listen! I am coming like a thief!... will not walk around naked and be ashamed in public.* This does not mean garments, but to be stripped of your ideas, your ideals, and all of the things that make up the complexity that you know to be *you*.

*happy is he who stays awake.* Happy indeed is he who clothed in the truth of his being.

The seventh plague. It is the last; the final. Praise God! It is when the spiritual aspect of you recognizes, in its fullness, all of the error perceptions of what you perceive to be your past. It is when you are finished with the Earth forever; with form, with heaviness.

*greatest earthquake.* Not of the Earth. It is the final destruction of the ego. It is the last vestiges of that great dragon [ego] that has ever held you from your holiness. And at last you will be free of her.

*the islands disappeared.* Islands represent division - of ideas, of feelings, and of the idea that there is a separateness - which goes all the way back to the idea that you can be, and are, separated from God.

*the plague of hail.* Represents ideas, sacred ideals, that bombard the ego and bring it down.

Revelation, Chapter Seventeen

*that great city.* The ego. That aspect of you that has allowed the ego to dictate your life - because it taught you to fear. In its beginning it was meant to be a helper to you. You turned your power over to it.

*the power has been given to the beast.* You told the ego to tell you what you should do and not do; and the ego did exactly that. All your perceived lifetimes your ego has been in control. It has chosen your karma.

*fornication with her.* The ego has become your mistress, and it dictates how you should live.

*the woman.* This is your intuition of the spirit of you, brought down into limitation. Your intuition will never lie to you. You have brought it down into psychicness. Psychicness is of the astral (emotional), not the feeling nature (spiritual). The day will come when mediums and psychics will be no more; for *all* will know they can know whatever they want to know, directly from spirit, themselves. You have adulterated the intuition by bringing it down into the emotional body and turning it into psychicness.

*the beast will reappear.* The ego will reappear. Egos get together with other egos - an army of egos, like hoards of mice. Why think you it takes the angels from the realms of glory to help you live your lives?

*the hills that the woman sits on.* Also the seven kings: states of consciousness.

Seven hills are the out-picturing of Earth cycles. You have gone through 5 of them. You are in number 6, and number seven is yet to come. The ego has set upon these hills and ruled the world.

*ten horns; ten kings.* All the powers of the ego. Ten things you have yet to be; ten consciousnesses. You are just beginning. As you come into those realities, they will have their balance.

*for one hour.* Not earth time. A brief moment of power of the ego. One last attempt by the ego to keep control.

*the waters you saw.* The earth cycles; parts of your awareness that you have brought forth, experienced and allowed to go past. The changing of times on earth - the unfolding, as it were.

*great city.* The ego with her fears; with all of her error perceptions, and all of the 'thou shalt not's' that she has brought forth.

Fear has ruled your world. It has been used in the name of God to destroy whole races of people, to slay innocents, to bring destruction; ever seeking to destroy the human spirit (its only enemy).

The Bible speaks of business [men] several times. They represent the busy-ness of the Earth. They are those ideals, thoughts of the mind of yours, which are caught up with (physical) living on the earth plane: earn a living, sell goods, buy goods etc. The changes on earth [are] from changes within *you.*"

*fall of Babylon and whore upon the hill etc.* All refer to aspects of yourselves which you are meeting and allowing to fall away. Do not engage in battle with the ego, for the ego will win. To fight it is to give it power. The ego has to fight; it is the only way it can win. The spirit of you needs not to battle; it simply is. Nothing can destroy it. It is constant; it is forever. It is created in unspeakable love; limitless wisdom; forever livingness. What power could ever destroy it?

# Chapter Fifteen, Rev. Chap. 18-22

<u>Revelation, Chapter Eighteen</u>

*Come out from her. You must not take part in her sins; you must not share her punishments.* Is anything more punishing to the ego than to be totally ignored? To be ignored; to be thought of as not worth listening to; to have risen above it - a terrible thing, indeed.

*all the ship captains and passengers, the sailors who earn their living on the sea.* All of the fears; all of the sorrows all of the emotional turmoil that you have put yourselves through are being brought down.

*in one hour she has lost everything.* Triumph of the intuition coming forth.

*false magic.* Commercials on TV - 'buy, buy, buy; you need all this to please others; to please self; to clothe self, to hide self (don't go naked!)'. The ruling thing on Earth is appearance, and it is based on fear. Countries want to appear prosperous and powerful; people want to appear happy and successful; in charge of their lives. There are the corporate egos of transportation; of clothing; of [electronics].

[the] national egos: The ego of the United States is gargantuan. Also [the] ego of Japan, England. The fearsome ego of Germany (watch her), and the eastern countries. The Babylon (ego) covers your Earth.

*those who have been killed on earth.* Not physical death. Never fear those who cause physical death. Fear those who kill the instinctual part of the spirit of you, that has hope. Physical forms are easy to come by. But when your ego, or another's, tells you that there is no hope; there is nothing to live for, they are bringing about the desolation of your minds and of the very spirit of you, and cause you to not want to seek life, and the growth of your being - that is who to get away from.

Revelation, Chapter Nineteen

*smoke from the burning city.* Smoke obliterates clear vision. It burns the eyes; you cannot see through it. The ego has used smoke, so it is fitting that smoke should rise from the destruction of the ego.

*to worship an angel.* In this context it means to fall down and worship your own ideology; your own inspiration; your own creative ability. Do not do it.

*the lamb and his bride.* You are both male and female; the action (male) and sustaining (female) aspect of your beingness is a singular thing. When you decided to come to the earth plane, you reached a certain dimension and at that point you divided yourselves and came forth as male and female; hence the idea of 'soul mate'.

*the wedding of lamb and bride.* In the male, the action aspect is stronger. In the female body, the nurturing aspect is stronger. The recognition, at a point in your evolvement, when you bring together in a singleness, both aspects. The reuniting and balancing of the [two energies], male and female. Merging of the consciousness into one.

*rider on the white horse.* Your intuition without your emotions.

*blood upon the garment.* The life force, the continuity; the forever-ness of it.

*coming forth out of heaven.* Coming from the divine center of you, where your intuition is. Your pure intuition is the Voice of God. It is the divine aspect of you that knows all things.

*the armies of Heaven.* The collective consciousness of humankind to come forth.

*eyes of fire.* Pure discernment; ability to know truth from untruth.

*rule with a rod of iron.* unyielding (iron) to powers that would pull it down into the psychic.

*birds of the air.* Pure inspiration not yet brought down into form.

*eat the flesh of kings.* The lesser things will be devoured, or absorbed into the higher.

*false prophets.* The doom casters who are working strictly from the ego. Also those things of yourself that would have you believe an untruth about you, such as: your were born in sin, you are ill, you can experience death.

*the beast and the false prophet were both thrown into the lake of fire.* The ego has brought you down. Fire is purging; the consuming flame of Christ, of truth, and burns away that which is not truth

Revelation, Chapter Twenty

*tied him up for a thousand years.* You have begun your thousand years of peace. The mass consciousness is being raised up. In the next thousand years most of the souls born upon earth will be of a nature that will not know war; will not know hatred - even if taught it at an early age. You are bringing forth upon your earth a new generation of spiritual people. Some of these souls have never entered the earth plane, so they will have no soul memory of a past; nothing to lock them into the old ways.

*nor had they received the mark of the beast on their forehead.* Souls coming to earth who have never been here before will not have the memories of the soul to deal with, so they can rule with Christ; with a Christ Consciousness; with an awareness of truth. They shall bring forth a New Heaven and a New Earth. They are not wise, but innocent.

*the second death has no power over them.* No soul memory that they have to leave behind.

*threw him down into the abyss.* The abyss has no bottom to it. It is formless, and must be called back into form, by the lives of those innocents who will come into the Earth.

*a little while.* When the [new souls] will keep the ego as their servant; in proper perspective.

*Gog and Magog.* The subconscious and conscious. Into them will try to come the influence of the ego.

*after the thousand years satan will bring them all together.* The ego will be brought back into existence, as it were.

*fire came down from Heaven.* Inspiration, knowingness; the fire of Christ, zeal. Ego cannot rule them. It has no power; it is cast away.

*I saw the dead.* Not physical. The dead are those who are unaware.

*the books were opened.* Books are a record.

*great and small.* Those that have lived upon the earth in your time and those who will have lived in their time - lesser memories, because they have not lived on earth as you have. Their world will be very different from what you have known; very different. You have not a concept of how it will be for them.

*Then the sea gave up its dead.* Dead, here, means emotionally dead. The sea is emotions. You have great feelings. Those of you who have been greatly angered, felt great pain - rejoice, indeed, for great is your reward!

*lake of fire.* Death of the memory of the soul. Verse fifteen in the Bible is incorrect. If you have not lived and gained the experience that you have chosen to come and experience; to go through and to live through - then you are dead to the feelings that are brought forth by these. You cannot know something if you haven't experienced it. That is why you should not judge another.

*then death and the world of the dead were thrown into the lake of fire.* All humankind will have awakened to who they are and there will be a fullness of the spirit of you; all your experiences will come together in a great knowingness in you. No longer will anyone be unaware.

Revelation, Chapter Twenty-one

*a New Heaven and a New Earth.* Old Heaven and Old Earth: limiting, binding religions of the past; old ways, old thinking - all [will be] done away with; gone from your memory. Do not confuse religion and spirituality. The lessons and gifts [will be] yours, but not the pain of the experience.

*The New Jerusalem.* The God-awareness will be a constant, conscious thing.

*God's home is with men.* Isn't that wonderful to know? See what you have to look forward to!

*And now I make all things new.* Can you not see the fullness of the spirit of you, when you come into that state of awareness? Indeed you can. That is the difference between you and I. You are called sons of God; we are only the angels of God. Your position is greater than mine. That which you are, I can never be. I do not mourn that, for in the angel realm there is joy unspeakable, for we have never left that state of perfect happiness.

When you hear the God of your being say, 'Welcome home, my son', you will have come into the fullness of who you are, no longer a child lost, out in the depths of sorrow or pain. All of it is left behind. Forever you will know you are a son of God.

*holy city.* You are the holy city. the involution down into matter and your evolution back up out of it again. The alpha and the omega: the completed circle. It is the completed journey of humankind."

*Jewels.* Crowning of humankind; its homecoming.

*measure the city.* Accomplishment; perfect in every way; the circle.

*gold, amethyst.* Gold represents love; amethyst is also love.

*whose names are written in the Lamb's book of the living will enter the city.* The completed human.

Revelation, Chapter twenty-two

*crystal river.* The foreverness of you; the crystal river that flows on forever; the eternalness that you are.

*tree of life which bears every 12 months of the year.* Your supply is continuous; you are never without. This is true of you now, only you know it not.

*they will not need lamps or sunlight.* That is the power you have.

*will rule as kings forever.* Complete dominion over yourselves. You have it now, but know it not.

*The coming of Jesus.* This is incorrect. It should be 'the coming of the Christ. Keep that in mind.

*"I am coming soon!* "The Christ awareness within each individual.

*those who must go on doing evil.* Everyone has a choice to remain doing filthy things or to change. You, in being clean, help them to come up out of it. Just as another going above before you, brings you up and so on.

*If anyone adds or takes away anything.* No ego-based human can take anything away from God, or add to God.

*May the grace of the Lord Jesus be with all.* The coming forth of the Christ, from within every person.

# Afterword

The focus of this book has been Gabriel's interpretation of scripture. It must be noted that three of the seminars were about Jesus the Christ, who also quoted scripture. These seminars are of the greatest significance to humankind, as Jesus came to show us the way back home to God. The first seminar *Master Jesus* was not numbered because we (students) did not know other lessons about Jesus were forthcoming. Its contents will be found in Chapter Nine.

1. Master Jesus. Describes some of Jesus' past lives
2. Master Jesus II. Describes Jesus' relationship with his disciples and others he knew on a personal level.
3. Master Jesus III Presented by Jesus himself, explaining our spiritual journey and the mysteries of his teachings 2,000 years ago.

10/30/87 Untitled; Gabriel's first seminar

*Archangel Gabriel*
The greatest man who ever lived among you - Jesus the Christ - when he was about to leave his followers, he prayed for them, and for you (you did not know that, did you?). He was praying to the Father when he said,
"I pray for them. I do not pray for the world, but for those you have given me, for they belong to you and you gave them unto me.

"All I have is Yours; all you have is mine. My glory is shown through them, to hear my words. And now I am coming to You. I am no longer in the world, but they are in the world, heavenly Father.

"Keep them safe by the power of Your name; by the name You gave me, so that they may be one with me, as I am one with You.

"I pray not only for them, but also for those who believe in me because of the message. I pray that they may all be one with You, even as I am one with you. May they be one in Love.

"I gave them the same glory that You gave me. I am one with You. I pray that they may be one with you also.

"I am in them, and they in me, and we in Thee.

"Father, you have given them to me, and I want them to be with You - and in You; even as I am in You, so that they may see the glory that You gave me."

# APPENDIX

Author note: Listening to the original audiocassette recordings of Archangel Gabriel is exciting and rewarding. Also, it is fascinating to hear Jesus the Christ speak of his experiences on Earth 2,000 years ago. The reader is encouraged to hear all the recordings, some of which are now available on CDs. Also, many lessons have been printed. Refer to Sacredgardenfellowship website.

Untitled September 1988
Ascension and Transcendence 2/16/91
Beginning Ascension 101 11/20/93
Beside the Still Waters 7/15/95
Breaking Resistance Barriers 6/19/93
Building Spiritual Power 9/26/92
Chambers of the Heart 7/24/93
Decisions - What are They Really? 3/23/91
Earth Changes: Cleansing and Healing 8/10/91
Effective Use of Spiritual Tools I 9/17/94
Effective Use of Spiritual Tools II 10/8/94
Effective Use of Spiritual Tools III 11/12/94
The Fatherhood of God; the Brotherhood of Man 9/28/91
Female Energy 1/15/89
Five Gates of Initiation 5/20/95
Gifts of the Spirit 11/21/92
Holy Breath of Lie 3/27/93
How to Live in the Days to Come 10/28/89
Karma and Grace 8/1/89
Making Spirit Life Real 10/1-10/3/93
Multi-Dimensions of Consciousness 6/24/89
Opening of the Internal Door 9/16/95
Polarizing Energies 1/15/94
Prayer and Meditation 11/23/91
Questions and Answers 3/13/95
The Revelation to John Part I 1/25/92
The Revelation to John Part II 2/22/92

*Rev. Ellen Wallace Douglas*

The Sacred Garden 7/25/92
The Sacred Thread 5/23/92
Vibrations 5/25/91
What the Will Power Is 11/9/89
Windows of the Mind 3/18/95

# DISCOGRAPHY

Author note: Listening to the original audiocassette recordings of Archangel Gabriel, as he gives the wisdom of the ages, interlaced with earthly humor, is exciting and rewarding. It is fascinating to hear Jesus the Christ explain his experiences on Earth 2,000 years ago. The reader is encouraged to hear all the recordings, some of which are now available on CDs. Also, many lessons have been printed. Refer to Sacredgardenfellowship website.

| | |
|---|---|
| Untitled | 9/88 |
| Ascension and Transcendence | 2/16/91 |
| Awakening the Master Within (Jesus and Gabriel) | 9/21/96 |
| Beginning Ascension 101 (CD) | 11/20/93 |
| Beside the Still Waters | 7/15/95 |
| Breaking Resistance Barriers | 6/15/93 |
| Building Spiritual Power (CD) | 9/26/92 |
| Chambers of the Heart | 7/24/93 |
| Decisions: What are they, Really? | 3/23/91 |
| Earth Changes: Cleansing and Healing | 8/10/91 |
| Effective Use of Spiritual Tools I | 9/17/94 |
| Effective Use of Spiritual Tools II | 10/8/94 |
| Effective Use of Spiritual Tools III | 11/12/94 |
| The Fatherhood of God; the Brotherhood of Man | 9/28/91 |
| Female Energy | 1/15/89 |
| The Five Gates of Initiation | 5/20/95 |
| Gifts of the Spirit | 11/21/92 |
| Holy Breath of Life | 3/27/93 |
| How to Live in the Days to Come | 10.28/89 |
| Internal Awareness (Jesus and Gabriel) | 5/18/96 |
| Karma and Grace | 8/1/89 |
| Making Spirit Life Real | 10/1-3/93 |
| Master Jesus | 1/18/97 |
| Master Jesus III (Jesus the Christ) | 1/17/98 |
| Multi-Dimensions of Consciousness | 6/24/89 |